Big Screen, Sr.

BIG SCREEN, SMALL SCREEN

A practical guide to writing for
film and television in Australia

Coral Drouyn

ALLEN & UNWIN

First published in 1994
Allen & Unwin Pty Ltd
9 Atchison Street, St Leonards, NSW 2065 Australia

National Library of Australia
Cataloguing-in-Publication data:

Drouyn, Coral
  Big screen, small screen.

  ISBN 1 86373 732 4.

  1. Television authorship. 2. Motion picture authorship.
  I. Title.

808.225

Set in 10/11pt Aster by DOCUPRO, Sydney
Printed by Chong Moh Offset Printing Pty Ltd, Singapore

10 9 8 7 6 5 4 3 2 1

Contents

Contents   vii

*For dearest Kels and Liza B, great writers
and daughters; Peg and Mike who said I could,
and should; Annie, who can and will; Selwa, who made sure I did;
and the class at Wordfest who wanted to know,
'Where's the book?'*

Acknowledgements

I owe a great debt to my dear other half, Tony, for the research; the bibliography; the preliminary proofing; the countless cups of tea and coffee and the endless patience. Thank you, Snuff. Two very obliging writers, Henry Tefay (film), and Kit Oldfield (television) gave valuable feedback and contributed to lively discussions. Rick Raftos, my agent, gave me the perfect impetus for writing: he bet me I wouldn't finish on time. Thanks too, to the writers I've worked with, experienced and novice, for providing the questions that ultimately convinced me there needed to be a book to cover them all.

Introduction

The biggest-selling blockbuster book of all time boasts the unforgettable phrase: *In the beginning was the word* . . .

This might lead some to suppose that God was/is a writer. Certainly I know several writers who believe, as creators of sorts, that they are The Creator. All flippancy aside, the irrefutable fact is that before and behind the word is the thought, the idea. That's where it all begins.

Since you have read this far, I'll assume that you have begged, borrowed or bought this book (or are perhaps browsing, bewildered, in the bookshop), because you already have the thought, the idea, that you want to write 'pictures': that is, film and/or television. While they are two sides of the moving media coin, they require different craft skills, different approaches, different viewpoints.

Perhaps you are already a writer for another medium. Possibly you have always wanted to write, but relate more to movies than to novels. Maybe you simply want to make money and have seen enough dreadful films or television drama to think you couldn't possibly do any worse. Or you may well be doing one of the many writing courses available at tertiary institutions around the country.

Whatever the reason, the thought process is in place, the idea is now ingrained. So, where do you go from here? I could say that you buy the book, follow it carefully and then wait for producers to beat a path to your door whilst you write your AFI or Logie acceptance speech.

Ah, if only it were that simple.

We, as writers, are born with the talent to write. It cannot be taught or bought if it does not exist in some miniscule form at the outset. Still, it is only the first requisite for a writer. What is then available is a large range of craft skills which will not only enhance but free your talent for the business of creating a script. Having promised all that, much like the genie in the story of Aladdin, there is a catch. It is this: not all writers, even great writers, make great screenwriters (or even bad screenwriters for that matter). Writing for the screen requires another, additional, talent . . . the ability to visualise, to capture your story not in words, but in pictures. Sounds simple, doesn't it? The reality is that many writers never adapt to the screen—not because they do not have the craft skills, but because their talent is rooted in words rather than pictures. They simply lack that ability to visualise.

So, to save you the price of the book, and myself and the publisher the humiliation of your subsequent claim that you learned nothing from it (since your script has been rejected even by producers with the most dubious of credits), I have devised a two-minute test for which you do not even need a pencil.

Q: Do you, when reading a book, find yourself getting bored with reams of description or evocative prose denoting thought processes?

Q: Are you always anxious to get to the action, where SOME-BODY is DOING SOMETHING?

Q: When writing your story/novel, do you have trouble tearing yourself away from the main character, the main theme, in order to develop secondary themes and subplots?

Q: When you tell a story to someone, no matter how brief, can you actually SEE it all happening in your mind's eye, just as though there is a tiny screen under the skin behind your fore-head?

Q: When you watch a movie or television, do you find yourself anticipating what the character will do next, and growing angry when he or she behaves in a way contrary to your expectations?

Q: Are you more interested in 'active' rather than 'passive' people? (By 'active' I don't mean action per se, but people who take command of situations they encounter, rather than those who passively let things happen to them and who never allow us to be part of what they are thinking.)

Q: Are you a person who gets involved in life and shares emotions, rather than one who shies away from new experiences, preferring to be a spectator? (Or, if you're not, would you prefer to be?)

Q: When you are telling, or hearing, a story, do you want the embellishments kept to a minimum so that you can quickly home in on what the story is REALLY about?

Novel writing is a process of internalization. The novelist has the luxury of indulging himself in ten pages of descriptive narrative if that's what it takes to convey a specific emotion. The art of screenwriting is externalization. A specific emotion has to be conveyed to the audience in the split second that it takes for the character to feel it, and often it must be conveyed without words.

If you answered yes to all of the preceding questions, buy the book. Do it now, before you have a chance to doubt your own ability to adapt from words to pictures.

This book WON'T be written in American jargon for would-be Hollywood studio system writers; WON'T waste your time telling you how to analyse other writers' problems when you haven't yet learned to recognise your own; WON'T give you the talent to write if you don't already have it; WON'T provide you with a thousand and one excuses for not being able to complete your script.

It WILL, however, give you real practical insight into all elements of screenwriting, from recognising the right medium to marketing your script. It WILL teach you those craft skills necessary to produce a professional script and it WILL give you practical exercises to make sure that you have understood the WHY of what you are learning. Those things, coupled with your natural storytelling abilities, WILL eliminate most of the obstacles that beset screenwriters, and shorten the odds of your work actually reaching the screen. It may well conflict with some of the theory you are learning in a secondary or tertiary institution, but its purpose is to help you move towards being a professional writer, able to earn a living by combining art with craft. It will be of little use to the gifted amateur who would prefer to feed a talent with ideology rather than script fees.

In writing, as in all life experiences, the greatest gains are made when we eliminate all the negatives and accentuate all the positives. It's up to you to do that with your script, once you know how. And please, let me know what channel or cinema will be screening it. I want to make sure I don't miss it.

PART 1

Preparation:
Before the writing begins

1

Big Screen, Small Screen

DEFINING THE MEDIUM

You have an idea, an idea which you will develop into your storyline, which will ultimately become your script. Don't get too excited just yet. Getting the idea is the easy part of the process for a creative screenwriter. Developing it is the blood, sweat, and tears period. It's worth noting,. though, that the more work you do at this early stage, before you actually turn on your PC or sharpen your pencil, the simpler the writing process becomes. Why? Because you will start writing with very clear and predetermined parameters and these in turn will allow you to focus and centre your script so that there is no doubt in the reader's mind what and who your script is about,.and where it belongs.

'But that will stifle my creativity,' I hear you cry, or mutter darkly under your breath. 'I write for myself . . . so why should I have to lumber myself with all this baggage before I start?' The reality is that only highly respected 'star' writers can afford the luxury of writing solely for themselves.

I'm certain that legendary Hollywood screenwriter Lawrence Kasdan hasn't bought this book, but even if he had I'm sure he would not agree with such an indulgence. If you want to write only for yourself, then by all means do so—and keep the finished script in your desk drawer, bringing it out only at dinner parties or when people you love can massage your ego.

In truth, whilst writers and directors like to believe, or perhaps really do believe, that their artistic integrity is unassailable, decisions ultimately rest with the producer. It is not that this man, or woman, is a Philistine (more about that in a later

3

chapter) but simply that making films and/or television is their business. Certainly they have to love the script, for they will spend upwards of two years eating, drinking and sleeping with it. But, contrary to the popular song of the sixties, love is *not* all there is! There are decisions to be made about budgets, markets, medium, demographics, audience expectations, potential returns and, therefore, viability of the project. There are very large amounts of money involved, and some of it will, hopefully, be coming your way. It is these things, rather than how good your script is, which will determine whether your project ever gets made. Wouldn't you rather have some, if not all, of those decisions in your hands at the beginning, rather than someone else's when it's too late to turn back?

'But I'm an artist,' you're positively wailing plaintively by now. 'I don't know anything about business, nor do I want to. I just want to write!' Okay, point taken. But what I'm about to discuss requires more common sense than business acumen; it simply means trading introspection for extrospection—don't bother looking for it in a dictionary, I made it up.

Let's look at the basic differences between feature films and television:

A FILM costs millions of dollars to make; TELEVISION is cheaper, the process far quicker.

A FILM may be panoramic and huge in scope; TELEVISION is more contained, smaller in vision. A FILM is (generally) linear in approach, that is, it follows a specific path, tells a specific story through a specific character (or characters). TELEVISION is not so centrally focussed. Most often it is episodic and balances several stories, with an omniscient overview.

A FILM is viewed on a large screen in the dark; TELEVISION is seen on a small screen, often with the lights on, sometimes with a million and one other things going on.

It is this last, seemingly banal, observation, which gives us our greatest clue to the ultimate consumer . . . THE AUDIENCE.

THE FILM AUDIENCE

The film audience brings a defined *commitment* (the dreaded 'C' word) to a feature film. It has driven or perhaps walked to the cinema after making a conscious decision to go out; spent eleven or twelve dollars per head (plus soft drink, icecream and popcorn) and is giving up perhaps three hours of its time, including travel. It has an investment in your feature film before the lights even dim and the opening credits come up. It *wants* to like your film, otherwise it will have wasted its money. It is this commitment which enables audiences to suspend disbelief, or sit quietly through thirty minutes of film where little appears to be actually happening whilst you establish your first act. They trust you, the writer, even if they never know your name and give all the credit to the director and star, to take them on an amazing journey with your main character right up to the closing credits (which they probably won't stay for anyway). It is this willingness of the audience to be part of a shared experience which touches us as writers, even if we are unaware of it, and makes us want to write feature films. There's more prestige involved, and one of the reasons is because people are actually exercising freedom of choice by paying to see your work. That is why you have a duty to that audience, and we'll talk about defining that and honing that skill two or three chapters down the track.

THE TELEVISION AUDIENCE

The television audience doesn't bring that commitment. It has no investment in your work and *it will change channels* in five minutes if it isn't well and truly hooked—and it's harder to hook a television audience than a movie audience. I remember my dad telling me that people have no respect for something they get for nothing. Nowhere is this more true than with television. Not only is there an inherent belief that your work is inferior because it appears on the small screen, but you are dealing with short attention spans and diversionary episodes within the living room over which you have no control. Much like the monster plant Audrey Two in the classic kitsch sci-fi movie *Little Shop of Horrors* (Warner Bros/The Geffen Company 1986), this audience says, 'Feed me . . . NOW'. What you feed it may range from easily swallowed pap, designed to go straight to the large intestine, to a veritable banquet of dramatic ideas that is difficult to digest. Either way, your hungry monster requires spoonfeeding instantly in its chair. It isn't even prepared to meet you halfway at the table.

Am I saying, then, that it is harder to write for television than for cinema?

Not at all, but different audiences require different approaches, different storytelling techniques. You'll see in the chapters on writing, particularly those parts on structure, how your three-act film may become a six-act television drama . . . and how your first-act turning point (round about page 25 or so in your screenplay) may need to happen in the first five minutes on television if you want to keep your audience.

With that understanding on board, let's look at your storyline through the following questions and see if we can identify which medium you really should be writing for.

SPECIFIC MEDIUM IDENTIFICATION

1   Is the storyline visually panoramic and dynamic? Within your framework, do the actual pictures, the locations, the emotions that you want the audience to take away, matter far more than the words? Is the story told in linear fashion— that is, do we follow the story through a main character, do we share his or her thoughts and experiences as they actually happen? Is the underlying theme, outside of the plot, a journey of some kind—that is, a quest? This quest might be physical, tangible, or it could be spiritual, emotional or intellectual—the search for the 'Lost Ark' or for self-knowledge. Is what the characters ARE more important than what they do or say? Is there a contained time frame for the story . . . a day . . . a week . . . a year?

Do you need time at the beginning of your story to slowly introduce the characters and allow the audience to empathise before it sees what will happen to them? Is there necessary (rather than gratuitous) sex/violence or offensive language, or controversial subject matter which might be subject to censorship control?

If you answered yes to most of the above (honestly), then the law of probabilities is that your script needs to be developed as a feature film . . . although we'll look at the exceptions to the rule. If you answered no to any or all of the above, then we proceed to the next test.

2   Is your story episodic in nature? Does it cover a lifetime, or are there big leaps in time within the telling? OR:
Is your story more about an event than a person . . . are the characters themselves secondary to the actual happenings? Is it biographical or historical, or based on some current event? OR:
Is it a small story, basically contained within one or two sets

with one or two characters interacting and no clear-cut path or resolution? OR:
Does it weave three or four subplots together evenly, without singling out any particular character over another? OR:
Would it, far from being damaged, actually be helped by commercial breaks to help get you over those time lapses? Is it more about words than pictures? Is it a story where the characters, of necessity, will more often than not state the obvious? (They should certainly never do so unless it IS of necessity.) OR:
Can it be made cheaply because of its limited requirements? OR:
Will it work just as well if the audience is only giving fifty per cent of its attention? In other words, it isn't overly complicated in either plot or characterisation.
Could the story and/or the relationships be ongoing, without a specified running length for the story or a designated resolution? (Often, when you're writing, you will think, 'I have this great set-up, great characters, great issues I want to explore in my movie . . . but I don't have an ending!' Chances are you are writing a series; you just haven't realised it yet!)

You'll notice that I've used the word OR between the questions. This is because the criteria are not as clear cut as for a feature film and you will find, when your script is fielded out, that often there may be uncertainty even on the part of producers as to which medium a first-draft script is best suited for. However, in general, if you answered YES to two or more of the above questions, then the law of probabilities is that your project will more easily find a home on television.

Examining these specific areas is described as looking at the dynamics. In screenplay terms, the dynamics constitute the dramatic range, the highs and lows of story frequency exactly as with sound frequency, the excitement and visual factors, the rate at which it all plays . . . in fact all of the areas we looked at when determining which medium. These are the dynamics of a script. You'll hear editors and producers talk about the dynamics quite often, so it's wise to know what they're referring to.

Exceptions

There are two other major factors to be taken on board, and it is far better that they are taken on board by YOU as the writer, before you spend months of your time on the script, than by someone else further down the track.

These are *star vehicles* and *budgets*.

A star vehicle is not another Lucasfilm sci-fi trilogy! A star vehicle is a project which may well move from one medium to another simply because, for whatever reason, a STAR becomes involved. Two classic examples of the late eighties are the small love story feature films *Falling in Love* (Paramount 1984) which starred Meryl Streep and Robert de Niro, and *Stanley and Iris* (MGM/Lantana Prods 1989), which coupled de Niro with Jane Fonda.

Ostensibly both of these would appear to be basic telemovies with no requirements that necessitate them being on a big screen. One could imagine either film starring, in America, possibly Mark Harmon and Meredith Baxter Birney or, in Australia, perhaps Gary Sweet and Penny Cook. Strangely, the Baxter Birney/Harmon version of either movie would have reached a much greater audience than the feature films' combined audience, for a well-scripted US-made telemovie has a potential world audience in excess of one hundred million . . . translate that into box office receipts for a feature film and you would be talking about a billion dollars plus, thus making it the highest grossing movie of all time. Ironic, isn't it? But somewhere, somehow, major stars were introduced to small scripts which would have seemed destined for the small screen, and thus, the stature of the stars determined the medium, because the budget restraints no longer applied.

Could that happen to your script, here in Australia? It's far less likely, but let's examine a hypothetical case. You've written *Shirl and Wayne* . . . a simple love story about a redheaded girl who can't go out in the sun and who falls in love with a surfing lifeguard who is claustrophobic and even sleeps on the beach. It's a light romantic comedy—you're in real trouble if it isn't! A producer has a deal with the ABC and, say, Josephine Byrnes is suggested for the girl, with Gary Sweet as the guy. The budget is viable—most of the action centres around Shirl's flat and there are only a couple of scenes actually on the beach with Wayne. Somehow, before the deal is locked in, someone shows the script to Nicole Kidman's agent. Nicole wants to come home for a few months to see the family but is worried that she'll be bored with nothing to do. She decides to do the project with Gary Sweet. For the moment it is still a telemovie, but inscrutable wheels are turning within the producer's head. Maybe—just maybe . . .

Nicole shows the script to hubby Tom Cruise, whose shooting

dates in Seattle have been put back six months and he wants to do the project with Nicky—if the writer can find some way to make Wayne an American. Now your one-and-a-bit million dollar telemovie is a ten million plus dollar feature, and your writer's fee just increased ten-fold. The budget becomes irrelevant. The money can be raised on the strength of the stars. If you think it's unlikely, you're right; but ponder this. A few years ago Jason Donovan and Kylie Minogue would certainly have been happy, provided that the script and key personnel were acceptable, to be offered such a telemovie. Six months later, after they broke onto the scene as international recording stars, it's doubtful if a local producer could have afforded both of them in the one project.

Sometimes the *star* is the script itself. *Driving Miss Daisy* (Warner Bros/Majestic Films 1990) would have worked just as well as a telemovie, but it had been an award-winning hit play, and so it had already created a feature market for itself.

In Australia that is true of just about any David Williamson script, originally written for the stage. I personally always enjoy his work more upon second viewing on the small screen, since it lends itself so well to television.

Conversely a hugely hyped movie like *Chaplin* (Caralco/Le Studio Canal 1992) was disastrous on the big screen in spite of an astonishing bravura performance from Robert Downey Junior. The film flopped, but no-one can give an adequate reason why.

My own belief is that the film script was disjointed, superficial and too episodic to carry the audience with it on its stop/start, to and fro journey. We ended up losing our connection with time and place because of the huge time jumps, and we learned little new about the man, or the period he lived in. Of course the budget was far too large for it to be a telemovie *but* there was more than enough material in Chaplin's life to warrant a thirteen-part maxi-series. That, to my mind, is where the project would have sat most comfortably. The budget could have been justified (as was that of *Winds of War* (Paramount 1983)) and the time jumps and episodic nature would not then have been problematical. The story of Chaplin's life could have been explored more fully, justice been done to the enormous talent of the man, and the audience would not have felt cheated of their expectations.

If you haven't started your script yet, use the previous tests to determine where it best sits, before doing the test again with the additional criteria outlined in the following few chapters.

Exercise

If your script is completed, try the following exercise: take your lead characters and impose upon them your absolute, top-of-the-range choice of actors in the entire world. (Money is no object in a fantasy, so indulge yourself.) Now reread your script with those stars in mind, as if you have never read it before, and answer the following:

Is your script hampered rather than enhanced by personalities that could swamp it? Is it big enough in scope to warrant these stars? Are you, as a writer, going to disappoint a cinema audience who, because of the casting, will be expecting far more than your sweet and unpretentious tale of lost love? Are you in danger of compromising what you wanted to say, because the huge stars necessitate changes in the characters to people more charismatic, more worthy of being thirty feet high on a screen? Will you have to cut your script back, lose chunks of the story you wanted to keep, in order to give lengthened 'meaty' scenes to the stars?

If the answer to these questions is yes, most probably your project sits more comfortably in a television format—there may even be enough material to generate a series. Conversely, take the stars away and ask the following:

Is the story, the journey, the quest, so great, so moving, that it will be uplifting to the audience regardless of who play the leads? Try to put ego on hold while you answer this one; or the weight of your head could cause you to fall on your face! Are the visuals so breathtaking, and such a vital and integral part of your storytelling technique that the characters become one with the surroundings?

Does the script set a mood, evoke an emotion that, once set in motion, cannot be stopped until it reaches its natural conclusion because the balance of the story may be destroyed? Does the range of locations, sets, special effects that are *absolutely essential* to your story mean that the budget will be higher than you might prefer?

If the answer is yes to any of these, then your project belongs on the big screen, regardless of how much work might need to be undertaken before it gets there.

Examine every film or television drama you see. Ask yourself if it could be adapted to the other medium . . . whether stars and budgets alone determined its destiny. Or were there other, more genuine and deeply entrenched reasons why it had to be where it is?

Sometimes a project will sit comfortably in either medium. Often you can build that into your script and you are then able to play both markets, which may well make the project more inviting to a producer. I have a project with a producer at the moment who sees a third possibility, that of a spin-off on-going series. It delights me that he thinks I didn't realise—that it happened by accident.

And that brings me back to the dreaded, 'I write for myself'. Once you are experienced, everything you have just read will have become second nature to you. You'll have taken it on board and no longer even have to think about it. The same applies to the chapters that follow. They become part of a digestive process that functions automatically as you formulate your storyline. Thus, all considerations are examined on a subconscious or subliminal level and—whilst writing for a medium, a market, a genre—you are really always writing for yourself!

2

Changing genres for the market

There is a new gadget on the market at present, a computerised kit for labelling anything and everything. I personally can't think of anything more insidious, but it is a fact that scripts are labelled at a very early stage. A producer will tell a distributor 'It's a buddy movie,' or 'It's a sci-fi thriller,' or 'It's a sitcom,'; something that easily identifies the project for the marketplace before anyone has even read a word of it. It's important that we look at film and television separately for, whilst the possibility of crossing lines and shifting genres exists for both, there are vastly different determining factors to be taken on board.

FILM

Some films are exactly what they purport to be. Look at the following lists: *The Breakfast Club* (Universal 1985); *The Year My Voice Broke* (Kennedy Miller 1987); *Flirting* (Kennedy Miller/Warner Bros 1990), etc, etc—teen-rite-of-passage movies. They have strong underlying emotional themes, but their genre is clearly defined.

Rain Man (UA/Guber-Peters 1988); *Thelma and Louise* (MGM/Percy Main Prods 1991); *Rich and Famous* (MGM 1981); *Lethal Weapon* (Warner Bros/ Silver Pictures 1987), etc, etc—buddy movies; some action/buddy movies.

Basic Instinct (Caralco/Le Studio Canal 1992); *The Jagged Edge* (Columbia 1985); *Psycho* (Paramount 1960); *Lorenzo's Oil* (Universal/Kennedy Miller 1992)—thrillers.

Whoa! Back up—*Lorenzo's Oil*? I know, you thought it was a social conscience/issue story, and indeed it is. But clever writing from Nick Enright and George Miller, both extremely skilled, nudged it neatly into two genres, for the moment you have someone at risk, and a race against time to save that person—you have a thriller.

Other films are not so easy to categorise at first viewing. *Strictly Ballroom* (Ronin Films/M & A Prods/Beyond Films 1992) is a Cinderella/fairy story, as were all the *Rocky* movies. They belong in the same genre despite the diversity of their storylines. Basically they're known in the trade as 'feel good' movies.

It's interesting to note that our Australian Film Financing Corporation was apparently not prepared to invest in *Strictly Ballroom*, even though the film's producers were prepared to put up a cash amount more than equal to the pre-sale requirements, until they were satisfied by distributors that there was a market for the film. Perhaps the perception was that the 'genre' was ballroom dancing. Would there have been the same hesitation if the FFC had clearly understood that this was Cinderella, or *Rocky* (UA/Chartoff-Winkler 1976) with tulle? Far from being an offbeat, quirky, arthouse film about an obscure subject, *Strictly Ballroom* fits neatly into the mainstream formula 'feel good' genre—and went through the roof at the box office.

ET: The Extraterrestrial (Universal 1982) is a 'Lassie' film (the story of a boy and his dog). Henry Thomas/Roddy McDowell want to keep the lost alien/lost dog, but the grown-ups won't let them.

The major story difference is that there are no puppies at the end of ET. Despite my mockery, I love ET; I think it's the ultimate film for the child in all of us. The previous year Sean Connery made a sci-fi thriller called *Outland* (Warner Bros/The Ladd Company 1981), which featured spectacular exploding human heads special effects. Was it at its core, really a sci-fi thriller at all? No. It was, in fact, a western, complete with a shoot-out finale. It was 'High Noon in Outer Space', but the reality was that there was no market for westerns whatsoever at that time. And so someone, the writer, I would hope, shifted the genre without losing his story and the film was made.

What about your story? The script you are preparing to write? Have you identified the genre yet? If you have, are you worried that there may not be a market for that particular genre? Remember that your first asset is having a good story, but your *greatest* asset is recognising that there are any number of ways of telling any story without losing the heart of it.

Exercise

Let's see how this works in practical terms. We'll take a basic storyline—a social issue commentary—and move it through a number of genres without changing the heart of it, identifying the elements we add at any given stage. Remember that no matter what we add or take away, we still want the audience to identify with the same set of characters, and to take away the same feelings. Superficially our story might appear to be going off in very different directions, but we will discover that the *emotional core* remains constant.

We will be using some of the basic structural and storytelling techniques which will be explained in depth in later chapters. For now, let's just take them on board without analysis, since it's genre we're concerned with here.

Concept or story premise   Sally Parr, young single mother with a handicapped child (David, seven), and little education, struggles against bureaucracy, loneliness and the threat of losing her son to the Department of Social Services. In the end she triumphs and is able to give her son the life he deserves.

That's our basic story premise in less than fifty words. It should be noted that if you can't define your basic story premise in less than fifty words, there's a good chance that you're not clear about it in your own mind.

Genres

Social-issue-based drama: this is where the storyline most obviously sits as presented. The two key words in our outline are *struggles* and *triumphs*. These provide the conflict and ultimately the satisfying resolution. Here is one way that the storyline may be developed within this genre.

We establish Sally and her story. Young, lonely, a single mother without the support of a family network or any close friends, she is living on the poverty line. She loves her son, who may be physically or mentally handicapped, or both. There's an incredible bond between them which is compelling and moving. However, the pressure of looking after such a child is taking its toll and she doesn't know which way to turn.

The first major plot point may be something as low-key as a letter refusing her request for a disability allowance, or as melodramatic as a doctor telling her she has a life-threatening illness which requires immediate surgery. But there is no-one to look after David. Whatever your personal tastes are, Sally is facing a crisis. She, and she alone, must take action or go under. Sally starts knocking on doors, seeking help. All the Department of Social Services can offer her is to take her child away and place him in foster care. Sally, knowing of the experiences of other single mothers, fears that she will never get David back. She refuses. But now she has opened the door for the authorities to investigate her. They do so, and Sally panics, takes David, and leaves town. With no welfare support she is soon totally destitute. Faced with no palatable option, and with the daunting prospect of prostitution looming, she decides that she will no longer be intimidated by bureaucracy. Sally goes back, faces the DSS (who seek to institutionalise David) in the family court and proves that a mother's love can triumph over all adversity.

That is our story in brief. Of course, there will be antagonists and, if this is a mainstream commercial film, an ending in which our heroine triumphs, thus satisfying the audience needs. Still, what we have is an issue-based drama and, at this stage in its development, it could be either a feature film or a telemovie, in much the same vein as *Fran* (Barron Films 1985) starring Noni Hazelhurst.

What happens when we move it to, let's say, the thriller-genre? The key elements are suspense, tension and jeopardy. The stakes are usually life and death. Our first-act set-up may well be identical to the one in the previous outline, up to the point where Sally takes David and goes on the run. This would then necessitate condensing some aspects of act one in order to magnify the conflict Sally faces from her own trauma and the threat of the DSS. Once we get past that turning point and are propelled into the second act, there are any number of options open to us, as we will see:

a) The doctor discovers that his diagnosis is wrong. What Sally has is a highly contagious and rare disease which will kill her and possibly David and anyone else she comes in contact with, in a given time—say seven days. A hunt is initiated for her, but the more the search steps up, the more Sally runs and hides, a victim of her own fear of bureaucracy.

b) David, in strange surroundings, becomes separated from Sally and lost. Sally is forced to go to the police after neighbours report seeing him with a man they assume is his father, and the police fear that he is in the clutches of a child molester. A full-scale search ensues.

c) Sally enlists the help of David's father to avoid losing her son altogether. The two set up house, but now Sally discovers the man is dangerously violent and psychotic. When she runs again, she has both the authorities and a madman looking for her.

These are just three intentionally cliched suggestions which point out clearly that the second act is where the key changes will occur. In each case someone's life is at stake and there is a race against time, and yet our characters are as before, and our social issues, which have allowed Sally to come to this point, are intact. Also, there is an inevitable 'baddie' as antagonist, and the struggle between good and evil becomes more crystallised. In a) the adversary is a disease; in b) and c) it is tangible, in the form of an individual. The good/evil struggle, which is always present in a thriller, drives the action and provides the suspense.

Looking at all the listed options (and there are literally dozens of possibilities) we would conclude that, rather than changing the key elements of the original story, we have simply added extra dimensions in order to move to another genre. Why? Because our social issues form a catalyst for the action. What befalls Sally in a), b) or c) are direct results of her single-mother status, her fear of bureaucracy, her lack of support which lead to her flight in the first place.

What if we perceived a niche in the market for a romantic comedy? The prerequisites would be romance, of course, a male love interest, and a series of bungling and bumbling incidents which could well thwart the said romance at the same time as providing comic relief.

Again, our set-up in act one could well remain intact, except that we would lighten the interaction between David and his mother, play it for warmth and humour. Our 'woman-in-crisis' turning point need not be changed. However, by that point, we would need to introduce our romantic interest. The following are possible projections which might drive our action:

a) Sally meets (let's call him) Joe, a bureaucrat with a real social conscience. If that's pushing the genre too much into fantasy, perhaps he's simply a social worker. Joe is instantly attracted to Sally but she's too caught up in her own struggle to recognise this. There's an immediate empathy between Joe and David, however, and the latter decides to matchmake for his mum. When Sally goes on the run, David inveigles Joe into being part of it . . . or perhaps even runs back to Joe as a way of getting the two together, telling Joe (in a simplistic way that backfires against him) stories meant to paint a picture of a lonely mother which instead convince Joe that Sally is seriously demented, or an imbecile, or both! Joe stalls for time with the DSS, acting as a go-between for them and Sally, and David manages to bring the social worker and his mother together for a happy family ending.

b) Joe this time is a bum of no fixed abode who has been claiming, illegally, social security payments for a mythical wife and child. Sally sees an opportunity to get both of them out of their mess and foil the big bad DSS in the process. Joe moves in, but the two of them head off interstate when they believe the jig is up. This time Joe uses the name of David's real father. The ploy works and the three play platonic happy families, which Joe clearly wants to swap for the real thing. Realising that Sally is not impressed by his past or his present status, Joe pulls himself together and gets a job and a future, thus enabling Sally to return to school and get an education. When Sally is finally brought to court she is able to truthfully say that she is a respectable married lady and the DSS is foiled again.

Do we lose our commentary on the social issues at stake? Not if we write carefully. Our drama is now a light comedy but the subtext is still serious, and we pose the same questions, examine the same issues. Have we compromised our characters in any way? Not necessarily, although the individual writer would of course look for those elements in both Sally and David that were playable for comic effect; downplaying the negative and accentuating the positive (positive in comic terms might encompass such aspects as paranoia, lack of education, etc, which might well be interpreted in dramatic terms as negatives).

Let's go out on a limb now and propose that our story has to fit a fantasy genre. Given the subject matter, this is difficult, but not impossible. The prerequisites are the stretching of boundaries to encompass the unknown, thus requiring the suspension of disbelief on the part of the audience. We could well have a fantasy/social drama; a fantasy/thriller; a fantasy/romantic comedy. We could use any of the story progressions we have just been working through. In each case, only one element would need to be added, and again the writer has no lack of possibilities. It could be that David is 'special'—telepathic, telekinetic or whatever. Perhaps his 'inner voice' (lucid and brilliant, and thus diametrically opposed to his outer personality) provides a narrative for us; possibly he communicates with, and is thus able to command, animals. Perhaps he is an alien, a changeling. Or maybe Joe is an alien! Or maybe all three have known each other in past lives. All of these scenarios move our Sally story into the realms of fantasy or sci-fi and yet *we do not lose our basic characters or story premise.*

Finally, the arthouse version, as opposed to the mainstream or commercial version. We go back to our social issue drama, but there is no happy ending. The DSS tracks Sally down, hauls her into court and, with justice taking a sickie that day, proves her to be an unfit mother. David is taken away and put into an institution and Sally winds up on the streets. If I appear to be sarcastic, it is because I don't personally believe that anyone deliberately sets out to write an 'arthouse' screenplay. (More often it is the *approach* to the subject matter, mostly visually by the director, rather than the story, which determines 'arthouse'.) I can't even get a consensus on an exact definition, except perhaps that the film would be playing the story for its ultimate reality and truth. But whose reality? Whose truth? Undoubtedly the downer I have outlined above does happen. Justice does take sickies; the bureaucracy does crush the innocent; life does suck frequently; and Sally would lose David. That's a perfectly valid scenario. But life can also be unexpectedly kind; justice can have her blindfold off and her bifocals on; the bureaucracy can stumble and fall; and Sally and David can triumph against all odds. Thus we have two diametrically opposed scenarios. Each examines precisely the same social issues, yet from different perspectives, one negative, one positive; both equally valid depending on your viewpoint.

I have been a professional writer now for more than twenty-five years, and I still get a buzz out of the realisation that there is an infinite number of ways to tell a story, and a good story with strong characters should never be hindered by its genre. Try taking your own outline and move it through any number of genres. Give free rein to your imagination, remembering only this: you must not compromise the integrity of your characters or of what you wanted to say when you decided to write. Remember that your *story* must always be about a person or people, but your *concept* can be about issues or ideals.

TELEVISION

We have already seen that our basic Sally Parr-and-son story sits comfortably within the framework of a telemovie. However, our set-up would need to be shortened considerably, or else we would need a 'hook', a pre-credit or a first segment grabber that would compel the audience to keep watching. It may well be that we would start with the denouement: Sally is either in need of drastic surgery or about to lose her child. We would establish that in the first two minutes of screen time. Then, when the audience knew *what* to expect, they would (one hopes) stay with the drama to find out *how* it would resolve itself.

But what of genres with regard to television?

Where feature film defines its genre and thus attracts its target audience, television tends to work in a completely different way. The all-important word is *demographic*, the predetermined identification of a specific audience group in a specific timeslot. Because television is self-regulating, its hierarchy must be careful to censor specifically for the timeslot, thus precluding certain programmes from ever reaching an audience which they might offend. (That's the theory, anyway.)

Television programmes also limit style and content by neatly packaging stories into predetermined lengths and segments. So it is the format which decides the timeslot and the demographic, and therefore determines the style and content. Almost always format and demographic take precedence over genre.

Let's look at those formats available to us, define the boundaries, and see whether our 'Sally and Son' story can be adapted without having the guts ripped out of it:

The **telemovie** or **teleplay**   Self-explanatory. Generally of ninety-minute duration—one hundred and twenty minutes with commercials—the demographic is usually housewives and white collar workers, and the time slot is an eight-thirty or later one. 'Sally and Son' fits neatly into this category without any change to our original story premise, but it would also be acceptable in any of the thriller or romantic comedy forms we have discussed.

The **mini-series**   Usually of four to six hours' duration, shown in two-hour blocks and promoted as an 'event'. It has a wide demographic, mostly adult but across the whole social spectrum. It's a prime-time, 8.30 p.m. timeslot. 'Sally and Son' in its social issue mode would be too small a subject. However, because of the episodic nature of television, the basic premise of 'Sally and Son' in combination with any or all three of our thriller outlines could be worked into an exciting four hours. Moreover, the insertion of commercial breaks, and the splitting of the story over at least two separate nights, negates the need for a seamless marrying of storylines. Thus one story ends and another begins and, providing the audience is still involved in Sally's struggle and ultimate triumph, they will happily move with her from one story to another within that mini-series framework.

The **maxi-series** or **extended mini-series**   This is a strange hybrid born of the old thirteen-part, self-contained series perfected by the Americans, and the serial, with not only the same characters week after week, but an ongoing serial thread that is not resolved until episode thirteen. Sometimes that serial link is extremely tenuous. This format is shown in one-hour episodes once or twice a week, generally with the first two hours blocked together as an introductory 'telemovie'. It is designed for a 7.30 p.m. or 8.30 p.m. timeslot and its demographic includes teenagers and housewives, with a smattering of business people thrown in. Thus it is more up-market than a serial, but less elite than a mini-series. This new beast, a favourite pet of nineties television execs, provides long-term content with style and class, plus more time for management to amortise production costs than the old mini-series would allow.

Would 'Sally and Son' fit such a format? At first glance we might be inclined to say no, simply because we don't have sufficient material in our story to spread it over thirteen weeks. However, if you take our basic premise, and then compare it with the basic story premise of one of the most famous television series of all time, *The Fugitive* (Quinn Martin Productions 1963–67), you'll see the possibilities. There, Doctor Richard Kimble saw a one-armed man kill his wife. No-one believed him, he was tried and found guilty of murder, escaped, and spent the next three years traipsing from state to state, eluding the law and looking for a one-armed man! When you break it down to basics, it hardly seems like a recipe for gripping television, yet it was.

Once Sally goes on the run, we can take her and David anywhere and involve her in any kind of story, provided she is always at risk. Of course we would now be talking about moving our genre very firmly to a thriller, and our three thriller feature film premises could be adapted to form separate episodes in our thirteen-week ongoing series, with Sally's risky situation and the 'Will they catch up with her?' scenario hook providing the continuing story thread.

The **series**   Less popular now, it is a one hour, once-a-week format which generally features the same characters week after week (although not always), but without any ongoing story. Each episode is completely self-contained within its own framework, and includes the interaction and personal relationships of the stock characters. Crawford Productions pioneered the format in this country with *Homicide*, and *Division Four*, throughout the sixties and early seventies. It filled the prime timeslots of either 7.30 or 8.30 p.m., with the majority of its demographic comprising adults of all classes. Not until teenagers began to control the television sets and the need to keep them watching week after week for ratings purposes became paramount, did the serial 'hook' creep in and the self-contained story lose favour. Its major characters, more often than not, became the catalysts for our involvement in the story which would feature a 'guest star'. But since 'Sally and Son' involves us completely in that pair's story (rather than them being the means by which we are involved with some other character's story). Since their story is episodic and ongoing, we can say that 'Sally and Son' won't ever sit comfortably in this format, no matter what the genre.

The serial   Lower budget in terms of cost per hour, it has now, with one or two notable exceptions, become the domain of gorgeous hunks and pop singing actorines.

In the many years during which I created the stories and characters for *Prisoner* (Network Ten/Grundy Organisation 1979–86), we prided ourselves on breaking new ground in issue storytelling and producing gritty realistic drama on an unheard of two-hour-a-week basis. Sadly, television serial drama has regressed rather than progressed in this area, with the exception of *A Country Practice* (JNP Productions/Seven Network 1983–93) which now has its own second generation of viewers and has just, as I write, changed channels. The demographic for serial drama is determined by the timeslot, which can be as early as 5 p.m. or as late (at the time of writing) as 7.30 p.m., it seems to be largely young girls aged between twelve and sixteen, with a small percentage of housewives and shift workers included. The serial is always about a group of people and how they interact. There are rules laid down as to the stock character meld and the function of each (see Chapter 14: Writing soap without getting your hands dirty) and very definite prerequisites in storytelling techniques. 'Sally and Son' doesn't meet any of them, so we can safely eliminate this format. (Interestingly, serials are usually an amalgam of any number of genres at a given time, since multiple storylines play concurrently and are interwoven. Thus you can be following a thriller in one scene, followed by comedy relief, even farce, followed by social drama—a bizarre concept that is peculiar to serials.)

The situation comedy   (or *sitcom* as it's more commonly known): Comedy is still drama. It is simply the antithesis of

tragedy. However, the industry defines the two as being opposite
in terms of programming. Sitcoms are of thirty-minute duration
and generally fill the 7.30–8.30 p.m. timeslot. The demographic
is varied, depending on the content and philosophy of the
programme (I think it's unlikely that *Hey Dad* (Gary Reilly
Prods/Seven Network 1987–) fans are also *Fawlty Towers*
(BBC 1975–76) freaks!). The premise is simple. Create a set of
characters with varying viewpoints that will inevitably lead to
comical conflict; put them into a confined habitat week after
week (a house, a newsroom, a cafe, an island) and let them
interact to a given situation with varying degrees of individual
hysteria. Whilst the premise is simple, the execution of it is
extraordinarily difficult, hence so many poor sitcoms. A sitcom
relies almost entirely on the character strengths of its major
protagonists. It's unlikely that either Sally or David, as currently
conceived, could be broadened enough to provide us with the
necessary comical conflict we would need to generate. There is
a glimmer somewhere at the back of my mind which says that
if Sally were feistier, prepared to take on the system and con it
for all its worth, she could become the archetypal 'little battler'
besting 'big brother' and we could examine all those social issues
concerning single mothers and welfare in satirical fashion.
Ultimately, though, I would put this format in the too-hard
basket.

The **docu-drama**   This format makes for compelling viewing,
as in our own *Joh's Jury* (Southern Star 1992) or the very first
production in the genre, *Cathy Come Home* (Granada TV 1966),
made in Britain. Mostly the drama is based on an actual event,
or a compilation of facts, or uses dramatic techniques, rather
than straight documentary narrative to examine an issue-based
subject. It is an adult concept with a largely white-collar demographic and is a format rarely seen on the commercial networks.
Actors generally workshop the scenario, or storyline, after it has
been carefully structured by the writer, and much of the dialogue
is improvised, that is, workshopped, between the actors and the
writer. Would 'Sally and Son' fit this format? Absolutely! In fact,
if this was my project, rather than our paradigm, this is precisely
the format and the genre I would be looking at. It would give
me the most scope, as a writer, to put those social issues I am
concerned with under a microscope and dissect them, whilst
still allowing me the dramatic licence of emotional involvement
for myself and the audience with the very real and vulnerable
mother-and-son characters.

Children's drama   Last, but by no means least, for it requires special skills of its own. This may be a one-off, or a series. For a project to qualify for a 'C' classification, it must meet the standards of the Australian Children's Television Foundation, and those guidelines are available to any would-be children's writer. Briefly, they require that the subject be relevant and identifiable by the proposed audience, and that it incorporate the child's vision and viewpoint rather than imposing an adult viewpoint upon the child. It should also stimulate the imagination and, depending upon the age group, be thought provoking. 'Sally and Son' would seem at first glance not to be children's fare. But what if it were, instead 'David's Mum'? Couldn't we examine the same issues, tell the same story, from a child's point of view, allowing David to talk to other children?

Would the story's adult concepts preclude this? I don't think so. Thousands of children in the viewing audience would identify with David's predicament. They don't fully understand the concepts, but they know they exist. If the perception of the child were the focal point for our storytelling, mightn't we get a chance to look at all those issues through a child's eyes, and see our welfare state, with all its anomalies, from his or her emotional viewpoint, and say something that's never been said before about how kids cope with their parents' pain and trauma? You bet your little cotton socks we would. Whether we could resist indulging ourselves politically, and remember to bear in mind that our primary duty with this story is to entertain, is another matter entirely.

Finally, a word of warning about our subject matter, or your subject matter, for any screen (big/small) play. It's wonderful to feel passionately about a subject. You shouldn't be writing unless you have something to say. But remember, film and television are both *entertainment* mediums. You should never forget that for a single minute.

3

Who wants what— and who gets it?

It is important for you, as the writer, to identify your own wants and needs from your script before you place it either trustingly or cynically into other hands.

Inevitably each person along the chain of production will bring a separate agenda, and a whole new set of wants and needs, to your script. Some of these may be easily accommodated without you compromising yourself as a writer. Some will not. Be very certain of what you are prepared to give up, and what you will stand up and fight for, even at the risk of having your project shelved. For each individual the compromises will be different, but you will find it hard, if you are truly a creative writer, to watch something bastardised and unrecognisable that bears your name and say with any degree of honesty, 'I got the money, I got the credit. They're all that count.'

What are your wants and needs? Probably any combination of the following: to be heard; to express your viewpoint; to enlighten; to entertain; to influence or change opinion; to evoke emotional responses; to go where no man has ever gone before (without having to join the cast of *Star Trek*); to use screen drama as a means of exorcising your own personal demons; to break new ground in storytelling; to have a credit on a major film or television production; to make lots of money (or at least make a living); to create; to be part of a medium that you love through the only means available to you; to get to see your favourite actor play out your fantasies; to direct (writing your own script seems like the quickest way in); to see how film/television is made; to *write*, because some small voice inside your head that is driving you crazy tells you that's what you were meant to do.

Ultimately, simply by finishing your script, you will have fulfilled your most overwhelming want and need. You have written. You are a writer. Whether or not you are ever a produced writer is a totally different matter. Most certainly, if you are, you will have had to sacrifice many of your preconceived wants and needs to the whims (funny how other people's wants and needs are whims, yours never are) of those on the assembly line to production, whose role could be argued to be passive, or at very best interpretive, whilst your role is the truly creative, ergo active, one.

Then, there is the audience, faceless, nameless, who has done none of the work but expects to reap the major benefit. It's very easy for the writer, especially a new writer, to hate the audience, or at least have contempt for it. It's even easier to simply ignore it, pretend it doesn't exist. But, if there were to be a writer's gospel, it could well start, 'Verily I say unto you, love your audience, for without it you are truly an hollow writer'.

Let's look at each stage of this assembly line as a means of minimising your own compromises.

The producer is most likely to be the first influence (and often the last) over your script. Therefore it needs to look clean and be properly presented and formatted before one will even look at it (see Chapter 11). Beyond that, the producer wants and needs a viable product, something achievable, so don't confess that your very first attempt at screenwriting is a forty-million-dollar sci-fi thriller set in Los Angeles with Clint Eastwood and Michelle Pfeiffer in the leads, particularly if said producer's credits are all low-budget, small-cast character pieces, set in the western suburbs. Any producer also wants to know what the 'hook' is—what is so special about this film that he/she can pitch to money people (including the FFC), a choice director, a star, a distributor? Moreover, there is a need to know what your commitment is to him or her, if they commit to you, as opposed to your commitment to the script. Don't say you'll change anything a producer wants (genre, character, storyline, budget, concept and theme) unless you are really prepared to do so. Later on, when you dig your heels in and refuse to budge, you'll be considered difficult. The producer also wants to know how this screenplay will make money, how it can be marketed, what's in it for him or her? That doesn't mean your script won't be loved. It simply means that film making and television are businesses, not charitable institutions. Whilst the producer may be keen to keep an Australian identity in your project, it is nevertheless true that this needs to be carefully balanced.

Anything so overtly Australian as to be inaccessible to an international audience (this particularly applies to use of the vernacular) is going to be disadvantaged. Remember, too, that the producer's agenda is influenced by those who follow in the chain, and is constantly shifting.

This brings us to the director, who wants a subject which is exciting in visual terms, a subject which does not dictate or limit the directorial vision by locking down everything too precisely or suggesting every shot, which gives him or her free interpretive rein, which is a quest, a journey, with characters whose souls can be captured in the camera's lens. Most directors in film also want input into the script, and often a shared writer's credit. Be both aware and wary. If you are lucky, the director will share your vision. If not, what appears on the screen will be the director's viewpoint, not yours. Ideally the writer, the producer and the director should all have the same vision, and be making the same film. It is alarming how many films in Australia are disastrous flops because the three major contributors had totally different visions which never melded into a cohesive work.

It's desirable to have a contract which gives you the right to have input at all creative levels, but it's seldom attainable for new writers unless you are lucky enough to have a hot agent and a project which both producer and director would kill for. It is also wise to remember that large doses of ego from either of the above, or even yourself as writer, are going to alter the agenda considerably, and influence the stakes.

The actor, who may well be a 'star', either local or overseas, has a different agenda with regards to the script, but at least in this case it is more clear cut and unlikely to waver. Whatever negotiations regarding money, billing, and perks, may ensue between the producer and actor (especially if the actor's name is an integral part of securing a pre-sale and finance), you will find, as the writer, that all actors have the same concerns about the script. These incorporate, but are not limited to, the following:

Is the character fully rounded? Am I able to approach this role knowing I will be playing a flesh and blood person? What motivates the character? What is there I don't know about the character's past that I need to? Where is the story going, and who is driving it? If this character is repellent, can I still believe and find something of worth in this person I have to play? Is there room for me to move and grow within the parameters of the character? Is this a good career move?

Self-absorption is a necessary tool of the actor, so it isn't surprising that the actor's concerns are largely personal. Once the actor undertakes to play the role, that self-absorption is translated into total absorption in the character you have created on paper, but into which the actor will breathe life.

The financier has a different agenda again. Films and television in Australia are financed in a number of ways, but one thing is true of all of them. Once your script gets to the point of being financed, it stops being art, a creation, and becomes simply a product, a commodity. As such, it has to be sold like any other product. Moreover, it must be able to be produced cheaply enough to guarantee a return on the initial investment. So, financiers require an instantly identifiable market which will provide returns; a budget which seems cost effective in terms of realising those returns, and a package of key personnel with the desired levels of experience to guarantee that the product will be manufactured on time and at a price as promised.

Financiers may be banks; companies with off-shore money; the occasional individual; stockbrokers raising funds through prospectuses; the Film Funding Corporation and, to a lesser degree, individual state film authorities. In ninety-nine out of every hundred productions, regardless of budget, the financiers require a pre-sale—that is, a written commitment from either a film distributor or a television network, in Australia or overseas, to pay X amount of dollars for the rights to show the completed production.

So, what do the film distributors and television networks want? Basically and bluntly, they want 'bums on seats', literally in the case of cinema, and in ratings points for television. Moreover, they require a major input and a right of veto over key elements in the production (script, writer, star, director, etc) despite the fact that their pre-sale, or financial investment, can be as little as fifteen per cent and is generally not more than forty per cent of the total production budget. So, the subject matter must have an identifiable audience; the production must be easily marketable, which means that the story should not be so convoluted as to be impossible to describe; the production must find a comfortable place in the market, fitting neatly into a timeslot or a classification, and also meeting (in the case of television) local content requirements.

All of this effort, everything the key personnel have worked towards, every concession you have made as writer, is useless if it doesn't satisfy the wants and needs of the consumer—known to us as *The Audience*.

What does the audience want? The responses will vary according to the demographic, which we have discussed before, and you will remember that we talked about audience commitment in Chapter 1. Basically though, audience expectations are different to audience commitment, and there are constants, no matter what the demographic is for your particular script. One of these constants is—it wants its money's worth. That might be defined as the price of a cinema ticket, or the investment of time in sitting down to watch the television. And you, and every other person involved in the production process, have an obligation (even if it is not at a conscious level) to give it its money's worth. This means understanding what your audience is likely to be, identifying its expectations, and then meeting them. Now some people will dismiss this as formula writing, but that, in my opinion, is self-indulgent claptrap. Without an audience, your work has no market, no matter how well intentioned it might be. A doctor or pharmaceutical company would not say, 'This medicine looks and tastes absolutely disgusting and it will make you throw up, but drink it anyway'. They would attempt to find some way of dressing the medicine up to look and taste more palatable in the hope that the patient would take it more willingly and it could perform the function for which it was intended. But it is still the same medicine.

Once you recognise that different audiences have different expectations, you won't find it hard to meet them in your writing without compromising your script.

Most audiences, whatever their demographic, want a good story they can relate to. They want to be able to recognise the hero very early on, which is why writers automatically put their lead character right up front in the first few scenes. It's an instinctive acknowledgement of an audience expectation.

Audiences also want their heroes to behave heroically by the end of the programme or film, even if only through an act of redemption. Most audiences will accept a bastard who redeems himself before the end credits; few will accept a hero who turns out to be a monster at the resolution. The rationale is simple. If they relate to a character—take that journey, go on that quest, feel and care for that person—they don't want to discover that they've been lied to, duped—that they are poor judges of human nature. Audiences also want a satisfactory resolution to the story. Mostly this is the much bandied-about 'happy ending', but it need not be that cut and dried. What they don't want is for a film or television show to dangle a carrot in front of them—promising something all the way through—and then whisk it away at the last possible second, leaving them deflated and disappointed. An audience also doesn't want you to underestimate its intelligence. It may well know early on who the killer is, or how the film will end, but it is interested to see what tack you will take in getting to that point, for that is where the surprises will lie. The old Hollywood adage of 'Who gets the girl?' still holds true, but these days the audience is also interested in how he gets her.

Australian audiences in particular relate well to quirkiness in stories and characters, recognising it as part of their culture. Whilst they can accept, and love, the formula Hollywood movie with all its cliches and stereotypes, its glamour and power games, its violence and graphic sex without love, they balk at those elements in an Australian film or television drama. They accept that America is like that (most of them have never been there and so their perceptions have been formed solely through film and television), but they *know* that Australia isn't. Thus, whilst any number of super-glamorous, super-rich, super-power-hungry concepts from the USA have graced our screens and rated through the roof, every single local attempt to Australianise such concepts has failed. The Australian audience will believe a super-rich, super-powerful hero who is not one of them. The minute the film or programme is set in Australia, there are very different expectations. The super-rich and super-powerful fall victim to the tall poppy syndrome. They can be part of your screenplay, but usually they are antagonists and must be cut down to size, with the 'battler' triumphing. Heroic figures in contemporary Australian film and television are, without exception (unless there's a film I have missed) ordinary people. Nadia Tass and David Parker knew this when they created *Malcolm* (Cascade Films/Hoyts 1986) and *The Big Steal* (Cascade Films/Hoyts/AFFC 1990). *Strictly Ballroom* is full of 'battlers' and 'ugly ducklings' triumphing over the 'powers in suits'.

Strangely, this Australian audience double standard with the home-grown product spills into other areas. The script may be less structured than a Hollywood movie, the story take longer to unfold, the romance be less physical, the humour less farcical or vitriolic, and more laconic, the stakes not so high, the resolution not so huge or out of left field. We, as Australian audience members seeing Australian films and television, expect our films and television to be different because we perceive that *we* are different. We recognise our national identity, even if we can't always describe it, and we're too bloody minded to accept graciously being the product of a globular melting pot. As writers, our subject matter may be international, our dialogue mid-Atlantic, but our characters' personalities and the way our story unfolds (if our project is about Australians in Australia) had better reflect the truth of our national identity, or the local audience will let us know by staying away, or turning off, in droves.

Let's go back to the writer's wants and needs, if your head isn't already reeling. You can see clearly that a lot of your wants may be in direct conflict with those of everyone who follows, especially the audience. Now separate them from your needs, those aspects which are essential and integral to your script and to you as the writer. Do they meet the needs of producers, financiers, distributors, the audience? If they don't, can you rework them, put a more attractive coating on the pill, make it more palatable whilst still maintaining it as *the same medicine*? Perhaps you could, but your attitude is that you won't. What happens then? The reality is, and I say this without rancour or cynicism towards an industry I love, your script won't get up. It may well be the best script ever written; it could contain earth-shattering and mind-blowing ideals and ideas; it would perhaps revolutionise film writing and production for all time. *But it won't get up.* That is just a fact of life. An unmarketable script is an unmakeable script, no matter what medium we're talking about. Take that on board when you start to write. Separate what you want from what you actually need and be brave enough as a writer to discard some of your wants in return for the audience's needs. It's an altruistic rather than a self-indulgent approach, and it doesn't mean that you have to sacrifice anything except perhaps your ego. Best of all, you are doing the 'write' (sic) thing by your script—you are maximising your chances of getting it made.

PART 2

The writing process:
Getting it down on paper

4

Character function

IT'S ABOUT THIS MAN/WOMAN WHO . . .

A writer friend of mine suggested that my first chapter on the actual writing process should be concerned with structure, since it is both the major bugbear of so many writers' work, and the skeleton of every script. I then asked him to describe a storyline he was working on and he started with the words, 'It's about this guy who . . .' I repeated the exercise with several other writers, both experienced and novice. Each time, just as I anticipated, they started their story by describing a person. The reality is that you may have a plot going around in your head, but it won't ever become a script until a character takes it over. In other words, until you know *who*, the how, what, and why have little relevance. A novel may be plot-driven, event-driven, scenery-driven! Language has a life, an attraction of its own. Prose itself can take on a persona, and a writer's personality may dominate a book. But a screenplay, regardless of the intricacies of plot and story, is essentially about people. That's why the actors demand much higher fees than the scenery.

So this chapter is devoted to character, and characters. Certain truths will have to be accepted by you, or this chapter alone would constitute an entire book. One of these is that if your characters do not work, your script will not work, no matter how ingenious, no matter how visual, no matter how clever, arty, pacey or action-filled. Another is that if your characters do work, many other script weaknesses may be forgiven. If you're short on story content, a strong character can create action and

33

drive the plot without you having to lift a finger. If you're pushing your script in the wrong direction, a truly rounded character will turn on you and simply refuse to move.

'Uh-oh', I hear someone say, 'She's lost the plot completely. She thinks the characters take on a life of their own.' Yes, absolutely. I do. In my own experience, I have created at least three characters for television which took on lives of their own to the extent of disregarding the writer. All of them were in *Prisoner*.

One was the delightful Pixie, the airhead bigamist with old-fashioned morals and the innocence of a child. There are still Pixie fan clubs in England, Pixie T-shirts in abundance, and we on the show took to talking to actor Judy McBurney as though she were Pixie. More worrying was the fact that she answered us the same way! Pixie was a very real person with a set of values which were not mine, nor the actor's, nor those of any of the writers. They were her own, and they determined her demise. When the actor was ready to leave the show, the character was raped. Even as I discussed the repercussions of this with my storyliners, we all knew what the reaction would be from Pixie, a girl who was so moral that she married bigamously (seven times) because she believed it would be wrong to make love to someone who wasn't her husband. Pixie was traumatised by the rape, suffering a complete mental break-down, and had to be institutionalised. I wept buckets as I wrote it, thousands of viewers wept buckets when they saw the episode. Even today, some ten years later, people still talk to me in hushed tones about poor Pixie's demise. Some ask if she ever recovered!

The other two characters were both villains. One was a seemingly benign and kindly young warder who appeared to be helping prisoners to escape. In reality he was murdering them and stashing their bodies up on the pipes in the boiler room. He saw himself as an avenging angel, and I based the character in part on Anthony Perkins' Norman Bates (Hitchcock's *Psycho*, 1960). Soon I noticed that we would all become jumpy when we were discussing his scenes or storylines. I started dreaming about him. The stories started getting larger, and his blood lust more uncontrollable. He began to be a threatening presence in every scene, even when he wasn't the focal point. We would come into storyline meetings wondering whom he was going to kill next, as if we had no say in it. I had created a biographical profile, a back story, for him (mostly for the actor's benefit), and I couldn't get it out of my mind. We all breathed a sigh of relief and went to the pub for a drink on the day he was decapitated with a shovel by a prisoner, Cass, played by the accomplished actor Babs McMillan.

The third character (whose behaviour so traumatised me that I have completely blocked out her name) was a thrill-kill nurse played convincingly by Maggie Dence. I had met Maggie some twenty years earlier when we were both young actors, but I never went to the studio, never said hello, never met her while she played the role. The truth is I was shit-scared of the character and never knew what she was going to do next. Her back story was that the doctors she worked with had turned a blind eye to her frequent practice of euthanasia, believing her to be a compassionate nurse who was helping old people who wanted to die. Only when a relative kicked up a fuss was she charged and sent to Wentworth prison. There, we slowly learned that this pleasant, even banal, middle-aged woman, obsessed with knitting, was a cold-blooded killer. She was not mentally deranged, simply evil.

It was planned initially that the character would be a long-term one, taking over the prison as 'top dog'. But within a very short time something very strange happened, and much of it was a credit to the actor. The show's producers, the network executives, some of the crew, started to get the creeps whenever this character was on the screen, or even on the studio floor. Several of the cast became paranoid about staying in the green room alone with her between scenes. Two came to me quietly and asked me to please kill her off. Soon after, that request was made formally by the producers and the network. Once again, the character dictated her own demise, without any conscious effort on my part. She encountered a young social worker in the hall whilst taking her knitting to the recreation room. As he put out his hand, about to introduce himself, she stabbed him with the steel knitting needle, under the rib cage and up through the heart, just for the thrill of seeing the light go out in his eyes. She then went to the prison hospital and injected herself with air, causing a coronary embolism. Needless to say, she watched herself die in front of a mirror, the ultimate thrill-kill experience!

You know when the characters are right. As an audience you relate to them completely. You become a part of them—and their trials, their quests, their goals, become yours. You don't question or doubt them, and you want for them what they want for themselves. Or they truly terrify you, and you believe what they are doing is really happening and are afraid to look at the screen, afraid they will somehow reach out from the celluloid and grab you by the throat. As a writer, you become intimate friends with them, and you trust them implicitly to tell you what they're going to say next. But getting the characters right isn't a fluke, and it doesn't have to happen only once in a blue moon. It can, it should happen every time you sit down to write.

We all know instinctively what characters do, but if we define some of those functions, we should be able to tell when our characters are *not* doing their job. So: a character is the conduit for conveying the story to the audience; the character is the focal point in the plot, the person who does things or to whom things are done, thus driving the script forward and bringing it to resolution; the character is the means of conveying attitudes and emotions, and should always be seen to be undergoing some growth or change as new information (plot points) unfold; the character is a source of identification for the audience, allowing that audience to identify with both personality and behaviour so that they become personally involved with the character's story.

How do characters do all this? They do it through their behaviour, which can be described as a combination of the following: ACTION/INTERACTION/REACTION.

That combination, though not always in that order, could be said to be an equation for any screenplay. Thus: ACTION + INTERACTION + REACTION = SCREENPLAY.

Doesn't this formula suggest, if it's correct (and I don't blame you if you are sceptical), that the characters control, sometimes even create, the plot? In a word, yes.

Let's look at how this happens, and the various combinations that are created.

THE SCREENPLAY EQUATION

Character A, disturbed psychopath, goes to a supermarket (ACTION). There he meets the checkout chick (B), who flirts with him outrageously (INTERACTION). She then brushes him off contemptuously. Furious (REACTION), he follows her home and murders her (ACTION). The police mount a manhunt (REACTION + ACTION) but he plays cat-and-mouse games with them (INTERACTION). Finally they corner him and kill him (ACTION). As he dies he confesses to thirty other murders (REACTION).

Now that's a simplistic way of breaking down a story, and here's the interesting part. Every time we have a bracketed word in that story, the plot moves forward, or takes a twist. In other words, *every story progression or plot twist is initiated directly by the ACTION/INTERACTION/REACTION* of one or more of the characters.

Moreover, the story happened that way because of what we knew about Character A—that he was a dangerous psychopath. If our character was a happy-go-lucky, well-adjusted uni student (that may well be an oxymoron), the ACTION/INTERACTION could well have been the same in the set-up, but the REACTION would have been totally different. Character A would have dismissed B with a cutting quip, and chatted up some other girl and we would have ended up with a light teen comedy instead of a black thriller. So, not only does character A dictate the plot, he also dictates the genre.

You might well think, if this were your story, 'No, he doesn't. I set the character up that way because I had already predetermined my story and genre.'

Then try this exercise: create a character out of thin air. Do it now. Give him/her a name, age, personality, and a set of attitudes. Now, spontaneously, give your mind free rein in putting that character into any story. You'll find within a matter of minutes that you have half-a-dozen usable stories, simply by thinking of a character. If, however, you had started the other way around—that is, trying to create a story—you would probably still be foundering, attempting to put the plot together, and you still wouldn't know who was in it.

(If you are in a class situation, this can make for an interesting class exercise. It's spontaneous and great fun: four people 'create' characters, and the rest of the class puts forward scenarios for them, debating the credibility as they go. You'll find that an infinite number of possibilities and genres arise.)

You'll notice in that little exercise that while I asked you to give your character a personality and a set of attitudes, I didn't ask you to define where the character came from or what he/she did for a living, etc. That's termed *back story*. It may or may not be relevant, but it does not govern action. Action in the screenplay arises from behaviour, and behaviour is governed by attitudes, and these are an integral part of the personality. They may have been shaped by the back story, but they are separate. For a character to work you need to know what makes it tick, not where it's been.

When I set out just now to write the scenario example above, I had no preconceptions. I simply typed out on the keyboard the very first sentence, and from that point on, my dangerous psychopath told me precisely what the rest of the plot was. And whilst it is true to say that the plot took shape because every stage of the ACTION/INTERACTION/REACTION process was inevitable, it's equally true to say that the course of the story would have changed completely if any of the characters had behaved differently. If the checkout chick *hadn't* flirted and then turned A down (INTERACTION) then he would not have followed her and killed her (REACTION) and all subsequent events would have fallen over in accordance with the domino principle.

Of course, that's simply an example, and maybe I engineered it that way specifically for this book. So let's look at some popular films and see how character combinations work at a basic level.

In *Crocodile Dundee* (Hoyts/Rimfire Films 1986) a beautiful American photographer comes to the top end of Australia (ACTION). There she meets Mick Dundee and the two are clearly fascinated by each other (INTERACTION), as a result of which Mick agrees to go to America (REACTION). There he meets a lot of weird dudes (INTERACTION), gets involved with baddies (ACTION), realises that he can't live without the girl (REACTION) and finds her finally in the crowded subway, sweeping her off her feet (ACTION + REACTION + INTERACTION).

Pretty much formula stuff, executed beautifully, and it went through the roof at the box office. But the entire story depended on the interaction when the two characters met. These were two active characters who initiated the interaction, and it was positive. Thus the story moved on its natural progressive curve. But what if that first interaction had been negative? What if they had hated each other? Then the reaction would have been different, Mick would not have gone to New York, and Hoges might still be putting shrimps on the barbie.

In Jane Campion's much acclaimed *The Piano* (Jan Chapman Productions 1993), a mute Scottish woman brings her daughter to the desolate coast of New Zealand to marry a man she has never seen (ACTION). He meets her on the beach. Each is awkward and guarded (INTERACTION). When he tells her that he cannot take the piano with them, she is both angry and devastated (REACTION). From that moment on the relationship is doomed.

That is only the beginning of a complex film full of ACTION/INTERACTION/REACTION. But what if the initial interaction had been different? Positive instead of negative? What if he had said he would come back tomorrow and get the piano? Would they then have lived happily ever after? Would there even have been a role for Harvey Keitel, let alone accolades all round?

My problem with *The Piano*, despite its brilliance, is that I did not believe Sam Neill's character would not at least make a perfunctory attempt to rescue the piano, to come back for it, to at least pull it up the beach so that it would be above the high tide line. The character is repressed, yes, but not unkind, not insensitive. Moreover, he wants this marriage to work, and yet he quite deliberately alienates his wife-to-be before the wedding. I guess the scenario of pulling the piano up the beach and coming back for it was not as tempting as the prospect of the beautiful visuals of waves licking the piano's paralysed legs. But for me, the film lacked truth from that moment on, because I could not relate to its emotional core. Because I did not believe *his reaction*, I could not accept what followed. Again, behaviour should be determined by attitude and personality. It seems to me that Sam Neill's behaviour was governed by the back story—the fact that he lived a long way from the beach and didn't have enough bearers.

Once we accept that characters do, indeed, drive the action and even often create the plot, we can see quite clearly the progression of the equation in any script or film. But here is another interesting fact. Every key scene in a script is also a complete scenario in terms of that equation. Every key scene starts with an action (although that action may well be initiated off screen) which leads to either a reaction, or interaction, or both, in any order. Someone arrives somewhere, or does something, or tells someone something—all action.

You may have heard of this interconnection between character and story being referred to as *causal relationship*. But to many new writers that is just a phrase, something intangible, even if they can see the result.

Let's take this example:

a) A child dies. His mother dies. This is not a story, simply because the two are not interconnected. But:

b) A child dies. His mother then dies of grief. Now we have a story. The action of one is the direct cause of the other, thus the term *causal relationship*.

If we express this in terms of our equation we see that a) can be expressed as ACTION + ACTION. Both forms are the same, and thus there is no progression. However, in b) what we have is ACTION + REACTION = STORY.

So we can see that *two* of the three elements must exist in order for the story and the characters to progress. More simply,

we can say that the *behaviour* of one affects the behaviour of
the other. Moreover the phrase 'of grief' spells out for us the
attitude which was triggered by the first action and so led to
the behaviour which constituted the reaction.

Exercise

Look at any movie—preferably on video so that you can pause
it—that has strong characters. Watch it all the way through first
so that you have a good understanding of who and what the
characters are. Now watch the film a second time, with your
pause button ready. Allowing for the setting-up of the character,
make a note of where the main character first initiates action.
Now note the interaction, or reaction, for there is no set rule
about the order in which these play in, pause the video, and
create a new interaction or reaction (your choice) without changing what has already been predetermined for the audience in
the character. Now use the change you have initiated to springboard the story forward and ask the following questions: how
is the plot changed by that one moment? Is the outcome, the
resolution, the same?

Move forward to the next moment of confrontation and do
the same thing. Remember that you must not change the character.

If the film you are watching has truly three-dimensional
characters, you will by now be cursing me. You will be muttering
that you can't change the reaction or interaction without changing, however slightly, the characters. And that is the whole point
of the exercise. The characters, when properly drawn, dictate
the Action/Interaction/Reaction, and that does not leave room
for changing them without damaging their integrity. This is
because their behaviour is governed by their attitudes.

You will hear a major moan in the film and television
industry, particularly from producers and critics (an unlikely
alliance), about the multitude of scripts that don't work because
characters are underdrawn. To a degree this is true, and the
major reason is that the characters have had the writer's will
imposed upon them. They have been made to act, think, speak
in a way that the writer wants, rather than what is natural and
integral to them as individuals. Often they are endowed with the
writer's own attitudes, which may well be totally at loggerheads
with the rest of their profile.

In the following chapter we will move on to creating the

character and the back story. In the meantime I want you not only to memorise the following, but to type it out in large letters and place it wherever you write. If you always keep this in your mind, you'll eliminate most of the problems and brick walls that confront your writing. It seems like stating the obvious, but it is probably the most important information I can give to you.

The characters do not know they are in a film or a television drama. They do not know there is a writer, a director and camera crew—or an audience waiting in the dark. They do not know what is going to happen to them, or what we expect of them. They are simply living their lives, one day at a time, and sometimes we, as writers or the audience,.join them for part of those lives. But for each of them, it is their life—not ours.

5

Creating characters and back stories

IS IT ALL IN THE PAST? OR IN THE MIND?

One of the major problems facing you when you first start to write for the screen is that there is a tendency to define characters in terms of the physical. Thus we may be given a character description in a script that runs, 'Blonde, quite tall, twentyish, she works in a bank'. This tells me, the reader, virtually nothing about this person. Is she shy, an extrovert, sexy, full of secrets, angry, vulnerable, confused, psychotic? I have no way of knowing. And since new writers tend not to work with subtext, I, as the producer, or director, or actor, am relying solely on the dialogue to provide the necessary insight. If those clues are not forthcoming, in terms of the character's attitude in any scene, then there is no way for the reader, in whatever capacity, to know what the new writer had hoped to convey. Nor is there much chance of this character ever being much more than a cardboard cutout.

There is a process for creating and defining characters which you can use even for the bit players in your script. It consists of a series of opposites:

Familiar/alien
Active/passive
Physical (action, materially driven)/cerebral (thought or emotionally driven)
Internal/external
Positive/negative
Wants/needs (incorporating goals)

Are wants and needs the opposite of each other? Not necessarily, but when they are you instantly have internal conflict. Then your character may well be at war with himself or herself, and the quest, the journey, may well be undertaken in order to balance those things within. Most of us face this kind of quest sometime within our lives, and internal conflict makes for a very complex and multi-layered character. On the other hand, if what your character wants also satisfies his/her personal needs, then you don't have inner conflict, and your conflict will need to come from an external source to create the drama.

The word conflict, for me, is interchangeable in dramatic terms with confrontation, and confrontation is the basis of all dramatic writing. Whether you are confronting a gang of vicious drug runners, or the realisation that you no longer love your partner, or even a custard pie in the face, is irrelevant. It is still part of the action/interaction/reaction equation.

So when we construct any piece of information about our character, particularly when it relates to the back story (the past history of the character up to the point where we pick him or her up), we are confronted with the either/or choices of our list of opposites. At the top of our list is familiar/alien, and this stands in isolation to a degree because it is directly connected to audience expectations.

What makes us relate to certain human beings? Quite simply it's because we recognise something in a person that we feel at ease with. Intimacy comes through familiarity and, if you want your audience to relate to your lead character, there must be elements in that character with which the audience is familiar. It may be the way the person looks, or thinks or behaves, but there must be familiarity if the audience and the character are to interconnect. Conversely, but at the same time, we all know the saying that familiarity breeds contempt, and if your character is too familiar, it becomes predictable. When that happens the audience anticipates every thought your character will have, every move it makes. So, you have to create enough familiar characteristics for the audience to identify with, but balance that with large doses of the unpredictable or alien which give the character its individuality and remove the danger of stereotypes. Once the audience realises that they only know this person up to a point, they will become hooked on learning more. The attitude, 'I know what I'd do . . . but I'm not sure what he or she will do,' builds a sense of intrigue between audience and character, even if the plot itself is not based on intrigue.

But, of course, this is only a small element of what makes

a character tick. You'll find that, in no particular order from here on, you'll be looking at all the either/ors on the list, and each choice you make will more clearly define the character you are creating. Rather than trying to explain the theory, I'll construct an example and then break it down, showing how we apply the basic rules. We'll take our friend Sally. Her back story might look something like this when you first create her, since all writers tend to start with back stories (and some never progress beyond that stage).

THE BACK STORY: SALLY PARR

Sally is twenty-two years old, not particularly pretty, not terribly bright. She's never excelled at anything except being a mother to David, who has severe learning disabilities. Sally was born on a farm outside a small country town. Her mum died before she reached her teens. She and her dad couldn't communicate and she withdrew into fantasies. When she met Wayne, she thought she was going to escape her life. He left her when he found out she was pregnant. She was still only fourteen. Sally had the baby, came to the city and, after attempting to work as a waitress, went on welfare. She has battled ever since to make a life for herself and David.

Now, on the surface, that might seem like a fairly reasonable back story. We've learned a lot about Sally that we didn't know before. Right? Wrong! We know little of real importance, except that the character is an active rather than a passive one. She determines her actions. The decision to come to the city, the attempt to work part-time to support herself, the fact that she is prepared to battle to keep her son, all tell us that. But the fact that the character is active is only one factor in giving her a three-dimensional quality.

The actor playing Sally will sift through all this (assuming she is given that much information, which in most scripts she wouldn't be) and, instinctively, without analysing the process, apply the 'either/ors' mentioned earlier. The problem there is that her choices might not have been the choices you as the writer, would have made if you had understood the either/or process. Thus her interpretation of Sally might be diametrically opposed to what you had conceived but not communicated. So you, as the writer, need to know more about what makes Sally tick, how her history has affected her and, most importantly, what her attitudes are. Let's break down the Sally character, building only on what we already know from the back story and the story premise we set up in chapter two and see how we, as writers, allow our characters to tell us things we didn't know and which they (as characters) may not have been aware of. (Trust me, I'm a writer!)

We have already seen that what has been created for Sally, in terms of plot and back story, shows us that she is an active character. Therefore she is a 'doer' rather than a 'done-to'; she initiates action where and when necessary. Does this make her a positive or a negative character? There are certainly negative elements in the back story. She's not bright, not pretty, did no good at school, lost her mother early, couldn't communicate with her father, got pregnant at fourteen, got dumped, has to live on welfare . . . boy, on the face of it, this character sets new heights in negative aspects. And yet, despite all this, we can't tell if Sally is a loser. Why? Because we only know what happened to her (all of which seems negative), that is, the external factors. At this stage we don't know how or why she reacted to any of it, the internal events. We are not so much the products of what happens to us, as of how we *react* to it. So we can't determine whether the physical or the cerebral drives her, because we don't know (yet) what her attitudes are. We need more information.

So, what do we know for certain, as part of the *now* which every screenplay is, that suggests the character is negative? Well, she runs away, which would suggest a negative aspect. However, her running away is, in fact, a positive *reaction* to a negative *action*, that occurs when the DSS wants to take her son away from her. It's a self-protecting move, and thus is positive. A negative move would have meant the character doing nothing, or surrendering defeated.

Okay, we can say at this stage that this is an active, positive character. Given those factors, and the storyline, the audience expects Sally to be a winner, in spite of all her trials and her inauspicious origins. So we can see that even audience expectations are governed to a degree by character. But there's a worry already with this character in that she is too familiar and could become a stereotype. So we need unpredictable elements in her attitudes and personality, the 'hook' that makes her an individual.

Let's build further and look at her wants and needs. Normally this would be part of the creative process *before* the completed plot and storyline. However, if you have a script where the character isn't working as it should, you can use this dissection process to examine all elements of the character. In this case,

I'm drawing on all the material we have created for our paradigm, regardless of genre and format.

Sally Parr

wants	needs
a life for herself and David	a life for herself and David
a decent job so she doesn't need charity	financial and emotional support
an education	an education
the DSS off her back	the DSS off her back
to feel good about herself	self-esteem

She may also want a knight in shining armour to carry her off on a white horse, but may need a decent man to enter her life and ease the burden, making her feel loved . . . and aren't they really the same thing?

We know now that there's no obvious inner conflict. Sally's battle comes from external events which cause her to react in a certain way. But we know something else too. Sally is a young woman who has her feet firmly planted in reality. She has no unrealistic expectations; we know that she is pursuing, with determination, what is attainable. She also appears to be in touch with her emotions, since she's not in conflict with her inner self. We know from her back story she indulged in fantasies, which suggests a rich imagination that's being sublimated. We would need to explore further to discover why—lack of education, or self-esteem? The answer will always present itself if you dig far enough under the skin. Perhaps that one little clue--that she withdrew into fantasies (had dreams) which she no longer does (she put her dreams on hold)—is the real key to the inner Sally, and that's what you, as the writer, have to convey to the actor and director subliminally. Maybe, by using and building on this, we also create the material to counteract our 'too familiar', or predictability, problem with the audience.

So a portrait is being drawn of a determined, centred young woman whose dreams are on hold, who expects little from life, but who will not allow circumstances (the external) to overwhelm and beat her, despite the fact that the road she has travelled in life (the physical) could well have made her a bitter defeatist. We can see, then, how this gives us the pathway to the internal, the cerebral core of her character. From this, we can enlarge on the personality, creating a set of values and attitudes which are specifically Sally's. Of course, that doesn't mean that she won't express some negative opinions. Of course she will, she's human. If you look at your own attitudes and opinions, you'll find that they are largely shaped by three factors: your childhood environment; your education; your personal experience.

If we apply those factors to Sally, we know that she was born on a farm outside a small country town and lost her mother when she was young. So her attitudes and opinions are going to be in line with that background, the more so since she didn't relate well to her father. Her personal experience in the city would have added to those, but she doesn't have the education to truly enlighten her. In childhood we usually take on the attitudes of our parents—bigotries included. Not until someone we admire more tells us differently do we start to question what we are expressing. Even then, our attitudes usually don't change a great deal until we really start to experience life and learn that what we are anticipating is not what we get. See how, once again, the external colours the internal, the physical affects the cerebral, the negative influences the positive, and vice versa. Again, if Sally's actions and background provide the familiarity with which the audience identifies, perhaps it's something in her attitude or personality which keeps them intrigued.

All this seems horribly complicated, but it is really just a process for creating a *psychological profile* on a character, so that we know who and what the character is, rather than simply what it does.

No two characters are the same, just as no two people are the same. But it's interesting to note that you won't be able to make your lead characters interact truthfully until *you* understand what their wants and needs are, even if *they* don't. You'll hear some producers or script editors express this in terms of, 'What's driving the character?' What they want is an explanation of the character's primary wants/needs (goals), and whether conflict arises from it. And you must have the answer.

I keep saying that, don't I? *You* must know what makes them tick, even if they don't know. The rationale is simple. Everything that has happened to us has an effect on how we function, even if we are not aware of it. The most graphic example of this is to be seen in the case of dysfunctional adults who often do not learn until quite late in life that they were abused as children. Some may have forgotten the experience, but it did not forget them. Hidden, but not totally buried, in the subconscious, it became a major part of the sum of what they were and influenced all their behaviour from that moment on.

If you discover that you have a character who is passive, and you need the character to be active, generally what's required is a change of attitude. You may think that the attitude can't be changed because of the previous experience, because of the back story. Not so. As I mentioned earlier, there is more than one possibility at every stage of the character's development. It is the choices you make then that determine what we see on screen. Those choices are a positive/negative reaction to a given situation which then becomes part of the character's attitude.

So: Sally, pregnant at fourteen, runs away from the farm to the city. Fact. Now, if we examine this further, we can determine whether it is a positive or negative reaction. It's positive if she runs away because of her determination to keep her baby and make her own life. It's negative if she runs away because she is ashamed and terrified of her father.

Despite the action being identical, the reactions (or attitudes governing motivation, if you will) are diametrically opposed. In one the character acts passively/negatively, in the other, actively/positively. So, from a writer's point of view, when an actor asks, 'What's my motivation?' it is not the event that led to this point that needs identifying. It's the attitude, the reaction to it that counts.

Having told you how to make a lot of extra work for yourself, I'm now going to tell you that not all of this makes its way into the script. You are *not* going to write great long expository speeches for the audience, for that would be the epitome of really bad writing. No, it is simply that you will know your character (in this case Sally), and you will be considerate and gentle with her because of what you know. If you knew that your partner or best friend was terrified of storms because he or she had witnessed the death of a close friend struck by lightning, you wouldn't berate them for an outburst of hysteria every time there was a storm. You'd understand the behaviour, and you wouldn't keep referring to the background which caused it. And that's the key to good characterisation—understanding. The more experienced you become with characterisation, the less important the back story will be and the more important understanding what's going on in your character's head will become.

Exercises

1   Create your own back story for Sally, using as many oppo-
    sites as possible to what we have discussed. Write your back
    story first, then use the techniques we've discussed to exam-
    ine our either/or progressions. How does Sally change? Can

she still control the framework of the plot, the basic storyline
we have been working from, if she becomes very different?
Will the events stay the same?

2   Take a real life event, preferably one in which you and your
whole family has been involved. Was it precisely the same
experience for all of you? Define the differences in terms of
how deeply involved you were (thus its degree of effect) as
opposed to your attitudes to it. You might also look at your
siblings and try to determine where differences between you
in attitudes come from. Have you experienced different life
lessons? Were you closer to different parents and thus influenced more by one than the other?

3   Watch your favourite film or television show and try to
identify with the major characters. How much of the way
they behave is determined by what you, as an audience
member, actually know about their background, and how
much by their personalities and attitudes?

THE CHARACTERS IN COMMAND

Whilst we've heard of films and television shows being described
as character-driven or plot-driven, we know by now that the
latter simply means there is a strong storyline, a chain of events
which moves in progression from A in act one to Z in act three.
Our characters are caught up in this chain of events and will,
inevitably, control the outcome by their reactions, even though
they may appear to be helpless in the face of a story whose
ending has already been predetermined.

Once in a while, though, a writer creates such a strong set
of characters that a story, or plot, appears not only superfluous,
but something of a hindrance. The most classic example of this
is, of course, Lawrence Kasdan's *The Big Chill* (Columbia/Carson
Prods 1983). If you haven't seen this film and you are serious
about screenwriting, then hire it from your local video store as
soon as possible. It is not the greatest movie ever made. It may
not even be a great movie at all if one takes into account all the
elements involved. You may well not relate to it, or like it. But
it is a great example of how carefully constructed characters,
allowed to interact naturally without the writer forcing his own
desires and attitudes upon them, create their own story, complete with dramatic conflict, comedy, sex, laughs and tears. The
storyline, if one could call it that, is that a group of friends gets

together for the funeral of an old 'gang' member and reminisces. Can you imagine how dire it might have been if the characters had been badly drawn, and not allowed their own identities? Australia's Jocelyn Moorhouse took a similar approach with *Proof* (House and Moorhouse Films/Village Roadshow 1991), in which Hugo Weaving played a blind photographer. The plot, or story progression, was minimal. What was compelling was the interaction of the three main characters. Other films to use character in the same way are *On Golden Pond* (ITC Films 1981), *Driving Miss Daisy* and *Turtle Diary* (United British Artists/British Lion 1985). It is not a coincidence that the first two were award-winning plays and the third was adapted for the screen by (arguably) Britain's greatest living dramatist, Harold Pinter. Since stage plays are generally contained within one or two settings, and since there is little in the way of extraneous scenery, location, mechanics and props, dramatic theatre deals almost entirely with the interaction and reaction of characters to some action which we might never witness, and may hear about only in passing. So it's true to say that all stage plays are character-driven.

I mentioned in our first chapter the quest, the journey that every major character needs to make. In a stage play, and also in a strongly character-driven film, it is always an internal journey—a cerebral/spiritual journey in which the character confronts the truth about him/herself and/or loved ones and is changed, enlightened. In film the external journey—the physical overcoming of adversity by the main character—may appear to dominate the plot, but there is still an inner journey being made by the character. The plot may be huge—car chases, murders, aliens landing—whatever the budget and imagination will permit. But the end result is that the character learns valuable life lessons and is changed somehow, and change can only come from within. So, while we're watching and relating to the more obvious picture—the journey in the plot—we're also experiencing the journey inside the character.

In Pinter's screenplay for *Turtle Diary*, three unlikely people conspire together to release captive turtles back into the sea. That's the plot. But is that really what the film is about? No. It's a film about loneliness, about having the courage to escape from the prison you have built for yourself, about being brave enough to really live. One of the minor characters doesn't have that courage, and finds escape in the form of suicide.

When you are asked about your filmscript, 'Whose story is it?', be very sure of the answer. Sometimes it starts out being one person's story and ends up being another's, and that means your script has lost its focus. Nor can it be everybody's story, or two people's story, even if the characters appear to be given equal weight within the script. This can happen, and often does, in television, but not so in film. In *ET* it is not ET's story, but Elliot's, the young boy who discovers the alien. Your script is always the story of the person who takes the longest journey, who has the most at stake, who undergoes the greatest spiritual growth, who takes command of the future by accepting the past and understanding the present. The character may not be able to accomplish all this without the presence of a second character, often acting as the catalyst, but no two characters ever make precisely the same journey.

It would be helpful at this stage, although not imperative, if you could view the film *Turtle Diary*, since I want to examine it in some detail, and you will relate far better to what I am saying if you have seen the film.

In *Turtle Diary*, Ben Kingsley and Glenda Jackson portray magnificently two lonely people who are observing life without participating in it. I've had many lively and stimulating debates (or even stoushes) in workshops and seminars as to whose story this is. Mostly students tend to believe it's the woman's story, because she appears to undergo the most change. She ends up in love, in a relationship, though not the one most viewers expect. But this resolution is deceptive, since the changes we see are largely external. She is a passive character, hiding behind her occupation of children's writer, afraid to participate in life. She has always had a capacity to love, to be open, to feel passion; it's just that she has been waiting for someone to initiate her life for her. And indeed, that's what happens in the unfolding of the screenplay. She doesn't really have to do anything except be receptive when it happens. So she doesn't have to travel very far.

The Ben Kingsley character, on the other hand, is an active character. Because of a marriage breakdown he has deliberately, through bitterness, decided not to feel, not to experience, anything which might make him vulnerable. He has created his own prison and put himself into it, given himself a life sentence. It is much more difficult for him to break out, because it requires both will and action on his part. Therefore, his is the longest journey, requiring the greatest understanding and acceptance as well as action on his part. So it's his story. But it could never be his story if she were not part of it.

Exercise

This may work for you if you're on your own, but is designed
as a group exercise, and is particularly suitable if you are part
of a writing class or group.
    Watch the film *Turtle Diary*. Then, take the basic story: 'Three
people conspire together to release captive turtles back into the
sea'. Now, create three new characters. You know the story that
you have to tell, but you must not create three cardboard cutouts
simply to serve your needs. These three characters must be
living, breathing human beings, with complete back stories and
due regard given to building their psychological profiles through
our either/or list. The only condition, as with the film, is that
they are not previously known to each other. The most interesting and exhilarating way of doing this in a class situation is to
go round the class and allow each person to nominate a char-
acteristic, or a piece of back story, and create the characters
jigsaw fashion.
    Once you have three complete individuals, take your story
premise and rewrite the actual scenario structure in three to
four pages. Your storyline is predetermined, but the way you
tell it is not. However, you are forbidden to push this new set
of characters in any direction in which they would not go of
their own free will . . . remember, they don't know they are only
characters. So, as you construct the plotline, ask and argue the
following: how do they meet? How does the question of turtles
come up? Who initiates the idea of freeing the turtles? What's
the resolution? Who gains what?
    This exercise can take anything from half a day to an entire
week. When you have completed it, and not before then, see my
comment at the end of this chapter.

CREATIVE VIEWPOINTS—AND PITFALLS

Everything we've talked about in this chapter is based on my own
experience. I've learned that any writer can adopt the theory, but
how successful they are in implementing it depends on how
willing they are to give up controlling their characters. You know,
many of us are control freaks, that's why writing appeals to us.
We are able to manipulate people on the page or on the screen
far more easily than we can in real life. It satisfies our urge to
control, but it doesn't make for good, fluid characters.

There are other processes for creating characters, and it's wise to look at the problems each presents. So, here are a number of writers' viewpoints:

'I base my characters on people I know.' *Pitfall.* Most of us don't know anyone as well as we think we do. Most people are not entirely open. Many hold secrets we couldn't begin to imagine. They present to us an image that they think we will relate to. That's fine within the context of the script. One character may present to another an image to suit the other's perception, but the audience has to be able to see through this, to know that the character is recreating him or herself for a specific purpose. And the audience can't know this unless the writer does.

'I interview my characters.' I love this one. My answer is, 'How do you know when they're telling you the truth?' *Pitfall.* Once again, if you take this approach, actually asking questions of the character, it will only tell you what it wants you to know, or what it thinks you want to hear. There may be vitally important elements that the character cannot bear to face, which it is never going to confess to in an interview. Also, in most cases, an interview situation is a performance. You'll learn nothing much of value about your characters while they're putting on a show for you. It's when, as I asked you to remember, they don't know you're watching, they're simply living their lives, that you catch them with their guards down.

'I take different characteristics from a range of different people and amalgamate them in one character.' *Pitfall.* Beware of Frankenstein's monster! This is indeed a recipe for disaster. You can't simply dissect people and use the bits you want, discarding the rest. Each character must be a complete person. Exactly the same situation will produce a different reaction in different people, as we have seen. It's possible to combine several characters' functions in one. In fact it is often done for budget purposes. But to combine bits of numerous personalities will only work if you are trying to create a neurotic and fragmented personality for your character.

'My main character is me.' *Pitfall.* Do you really know you? If you can look at yourself brutally, honestly, seeing all your faults and shortcomings, then good on you. It's rare, but I'll concede that it can happen. However, even if you are that rarest of beings, do others see you the way you see yourself? I have a screenplay in development now with a producer. The main character, a high-powered media star, is based on me (only younger, prettier, thinner . . . but me). Assertive, volatile, no-nonsense, a sucker for a sob story, passionate, generous, unpredictable, egotistical, vitriolic, crusading, compassionate, vulnerable, intolerant, judgemental . . . Yes, I've worked hard on getting to know my assets and liabilities, and I gave them all to the character. What a woman! Imagine my mortification when every man who read the script (women loved it) said, 'What a bitch!' With few exceptions, men reacted negatively to the character, perceiving her to be someone I had never intended. That in turn caused me to question their perception of me. It also poses a philosophical question. Are we what we are, or what others perceive us to be?

Since this book is about screenwriting I refuse to answer on the grounds that I might incriminate myself, and that it is not part of the subject matter. In any case, both questions are legitimate. Which is the more important depends upon your story.

THE GENDER FACTOR

The preceding anecdote illustrates very clearly that gender plays an important part in your character makeup. It isn't so much political incorrectness as simple human nature. No matter how much we might rail against it, men and women *are* different. They react differently. They display emotion differently. Equality does not mean sameness, it simply means balanced evenly, on the same level, and certainly each has weaknesses and strengths that you need to be familiar with. Neither one is better than the other, but that doesn't make them the same.

Part of the perceived threat of my character was that she behaved like a man would in public situations, despite the fact that she was all-female and quite vulnerable in private. I tried an experiment with the script, taking away all female references, including her name. The reaction was astonishing. When readers believed the character was a man, they were all for him, laughed and admired his every line, his every action. Everyone thought he was a fabulous character. 'The bitch' reaction was reinstated once they realised that the character was a woman. Some grudgingly admired her, but no-one liked her. Moral: certain behaviour is acceptable, even expected, from men which is inappropriate in women. Now this has little to do with chauvinism. No-one who read the script is in any way chauvinistic. In fact some, including a male producer, are open feminist campaigners. It's simply a fact of life. We should be equal. We're not the same. And I, for one, am grateful.

So, if you decide to change a character from male to female, or vice versa, be very sure to take on board the differences between predominantly right or left brain activity, different perceptions, perhaps an altered set of attitudes and values. The exception might be if your screenplay were set in the future. Since the audience has no way of knowing how society will function, it will suspend disbelief and accept a woman, or man, behaving in a way totally opposed to the current dictates of their gender.

In *Alien* (20th Century Fox 1979), the character of Ripley, played by Sigourney Weaver, was almost androgynous. Certainly it could have been male or female. Yet, when the sequel was made, the writer went to great pains to instill in the character feminine characteristics, such as maternal instincts. They even gave her a back story which included her having a child. The only explanation for this that I've been able to get from my sources (and I can't verify it, although I suspect it is right) is that audiences felt alienated from the character. Neither sex could identify or empathise with her, since nothing about her was familiar. She looked like a woman, but behaved like a man. That was fine for the first film but, in a sequel which was basically her journey, it was essential for the audience to know her and empathise with her. Hence the sudden dose of female hormones. It's our familiar/alien pattern again.

In reality, a human being begins as an embryo. From there it grows and develops; it learns and experiences, and changes with experience. It is constantly searching for its own truth. That's how it is in real life, so why should it be different in writing? In this particular case, allow yourselves to play God, for you are the creator and your characters are your children. Just remember to give them free will.

TELEVISION CHARACTER

Can the whole of the previous section really apply to creating characters for television? Yes, of course it can. Then why are most television characters so two-dimensional, so sketchily drawn? There are two answers. The first is time limitations. A writer may work for six months or six years on a feature film script. That script might undergo anything from four to twenty drafts until everyone is certain that it fulfills its promise.

But most of television is about making a product to a budget and a timeslot, and that allows the writer the maximum of two drafts for a script. So, if you are commissioned to write for television, be aware that you will have very little time for character creation. Most of your writing hours will be spent making the storyline work and timing your script because it's running four minutes too long. However, an interesting side effect is that in long-running series the characterisation inevitably gets better after about the six-week mark. This is because writers, actors, directors are gradually getting to know the people they present on the screen, and so they are constantly enlarging on the range of experience and attitudes the character has.

Of course, this can backfire. Back in 1980, when I was still acting, I played a character called Consuela McPhee in an ill-fated soap called *Arcade* (Network Ten 1980). All I knew about her, since there was no back story and only three lines of character notes, was that she was young(?), fat, and worked as the receptionist in the gym. Like most actors, I was forced to create a back story that I could draw on to help me understand Consuela. I decided she was from the western suburbs, a tomboy because of her weight, full of jokes and always laughing to hide the pain of not fitting in, not belonging. That's the way I played her. Six weeks into shooting, the writers decided that Consuela's parents should come to visit. And who were these parents? A lion tamer and a fat lady in a circus. There was no way my western suburbs misfit could belong to these two showbiz extroverts. That was when I decided that writing was a serious business that not enough writers took seriously.

The second restriction on characterisation in television is character function. In a feature film there are no hard and fast rules as to what your character is, or does, other than those we have already talked about. Television characters, however, must be recognisable types that the audience can identify with in the first five minutes. They must also possess a recognisable function or purpose, and the character blend is almost always the same. (Characters in your film script must also have a purpose, but that purpose need not be identified for the audience, provided that you, as the writer, are aware of it.) Thus the viewer at home is quite adept at saying: this is the hero, this is the heroine (they're goodies), these are the antagonists (baddies), this is the comedy relief, the Greek chorus (usually the neighbourhood gossip), the victim. Still, within that framework of formula television, there is plenty of scope for the writer to draw well-rounded characters with their own peculiar originality. We did it all the time on *Prisoner*. All it takes is a little extra care, a little extra time and a great deal of love for what you're doing.

Turtle Diary exercise (see p. 52)

I've used this exercise in writing workshops all over the country, with groups ranging from the young graduating class of writers and directors at Victoria College of the Arts, to middle-aged hobbyists or hopeful writers attending adult classes, and associates from the Australian Writers' Guild. Sometimes it's been a four-hour exercise, sometimes two whole days. Always it has been great fun and provoked an enormous amount of class interaction and discussion. At each viewing I learn something new about the characters and their interaction. But never ever have I seen a resolution; a believable blend of complete and whole new characters setting those turtles free. We've had everything from autistic children to aged ex-madams and Israeli freedom fighters. The closest we've come is when the three characters mirrored the film's characters very closely, and that really is a cheat. So, if you have found an alternative scenario with a set of characters that really work, that really come together, that really relate to each other, and who could conceivably succeed in setting those bloody turtles free, I wish you would send me a copy.

6

Structure

A STRAIGHT SPINE, STRONG LIMBS

If it's true to say that your characters are the heart and soul, and probably the mind, of your screenplay, then your structure is most definitely the skeleton. Your main, linear, storyline is the spine and the subplots are the limbs.

Our initial reaction to someone whose body is deformed, even though his or her heart, soul and mind may be perfect, is to be repelled. We cannot help it. It's a reflex action and often we feel guilty about it and put extra effort into getting to know the person involved. If the skeleton of your script is deformed, if your structure is repellent, the audience isn't going to make the extra effort. It's as simple as that.

In drama we talk about the three-act structure as being the basis for any screenplay, whether it's film or television (although we'll see that in television, concessions and alterations are made). So what is this thing called structure that makes even experienced writers quake when the producer or script editor mentions it?

It is the dramatic blueprint for focussing on and conveying to an audience a complete story told in pictures. Why three acts? Simple. A beginning, a middle and an end. I'm quite serious. This method of dramatic storytelling was devised by Greek dramatists more than two thousand years ago, and it has never been bettered. Auteur film makers of the sixties tried to shake it, conceding that there might be a beginning, a middle, and an end—but not necessarily in that order. Few have made more than a perfunctory dent in the nature of the three-act structure, although many are still trying.

So, if it's simply a matter of your story having a beginning, a middle and an end, why all the fuss? Because the three-act structure is not an idea or a theory, it is a discipline with very strict guidelines, and most of us writers don't take too kindly to discipline.

There are already several American books on screenwriting which explain the three-act structure, for example, Sid Field's *Screenplay* and *The Screenwriter's Workbook*; Linda Segar's *Making a Good Script Great* (see bibliography). But, since we in Australia have our own peculiar way of approaching things (we don't just want to know how, we want to know why), and since most of us are resistant to the idea of being told anything by anyone 'over there', let's look at structure from our own perspective.

You'll hear more than one definition of the three acts. As well as 'the beginning, the middle and the end', industry people will talk about: the set-up/action/payoff; the introduction/confrontation/resolution, and the build-up/action/climax. My personal definition would be the set-up, the confrontation, the resolution—the beginning, the middle, the end.

All right, you say, I understand the theory, the problem is moving from one to the other. How do I know that I'm leaving the beginning and starting on the middle? What tells me that the set-up is over and confrontation begins? What if I've actually got some confrontation between characters in my set-up? Have I blurred my acts, or lost my structure?

These are some of the questions writers ask me when I'm editing. Mostly they don't recognise that there are structural problems in their work. Writers create screenplays to the best of their ability and they honestly believe it works or they wouldn't do it that way. The problem comes from the very nature of writing. It is a creative process which requires the setting free of imagination from the bonds of the mundane. Structure, however, insists on those bonds and imposes discipline whether you like it or not. So, let's learn the rules, just as we once had to learn the alphabet. Then, once they are second nature to us, we can put them aside and give free rein to our creative muse.

1 THE THREE-ACT STRUCTURE—THE SPINE

Our model would look something like this:

Act One	Act Two	Act Three
The set-up. The introduction of the main characters and the story. The raising of the main issue.	The development. The confrontation. The journey the audience makes with the character. The bulk of the story.	The ending/ resolution. The end of the journey/ quest. The climax. The 'who gets what?'

Now, if we were writing a play, there would be no problem. The curtain would come down at the end of act one and go up at the beginning of act two and the audience would know precisely where it was in terms of the story. Since a film (we'll deal with television later) is a single entity, we don't have that luxury. So how do we know where one act ends and another begins? And how do we connect them, sew them together in a way that is invisible? Well, let's be very sure that we understand what a screenplay is before we go any further. You may think you know what you're writing, but can you actually define it?

A screenplay is a story or plot consisting of characters interacting in a series of events or actions which may follow each other or intersect, told (in scenic form) in pictures.

Since this definition allows us interaction and a series of events which follow each other—a progression—then we should automatically move from one act to another as the story unfolds, right? Wrong.

Turning points

To move from one act to another we need an event, or an action, that *initiates* a change of direction and acts as *the impetus* for the story to pick up speed and explore new areas. This is called the *turning point*. There are two of them in any screenplay, linking the first and second acts, and the second and third acts.

The turning point is not the same thing as the plot point, although it most likely will be *a* plot point. Your script will consist of a number of plot points, all of which will keep the story moving forward exponentially, driven by your characters. The plot points may be part of the progression, expanding and building on what has gone before to constantly enlarge the plot and the story, and the growth of the characters. The turning point, on the other hand, is exactly what it says. It is a pivotal moment in the story when something happens that completely spins around the preconceived ideas of both characters and audience and takes the story off in a different direction. Thus we move into act two; the momentum of the turning point has catapulted us into a new situation, or action, and we have to go along for the ride if we want to find out what's going on. In act two, we follow these new developments, or progressions, still wondering what lies ahead. There will be any number of plot points along the way, depending upon the complexity of your storyline as it unfolds. At the next turning point your story will once again change direction through a single event or action which must inevitably lead to, firstly, a climax, then a resolution.

Now that we recognise what the turning point is, and what its function is, how do we recognise that moment in our own plot? Well, let's go back to our 'Sally and Son' model, as a social issue drama. At the moment we're concerning ourselves only with the turning points. Given that there are any number of plot points, let's examine them to identify the turning point, and work out why only one plot point is the turning point.

After setting up the character of Sally and her interaction with David, we come to that moment where Sally is told by the doctor that she needs an operation.

Plot point? Yes. Why? It adds an extra element to what we already know and propels the major characters forward. Turning point? No. Why not? The forward propulsion of the characters and story is part of a natural progression of the plot. We, and Sally, have taken new things on board, but the situation is still a progressive part of the set-up.

Sally goes to the DSS for support. Plot point? Yes, for the same reasons as mentioned before. Turning point? No. Ditto.

DSS investigates Sally and decides to take David. Plot point? Yes, but we're still building up our story, adding both dimension and dynamics. Up to this point we're still moving in the same direction, so we haven't reached our turning point.

Sally takes David and runs away. Now we have both turning point and major plot point. Once that action is initiated, a whole new range of story possibilities, or second-act development, is opened up, and we, like Sally, have no way of predicting exactly where it is going to take us, or how.

You might ask: what about the DSS deciding to take David? Couldn't that be seen as the turning point? Ask yourself this. Is the decision of the DSS the impetus for an *inevitable* change of direction for Sally? The answer is no. She could acquiesce, struggle, protest, but we'd still be following the same progression. What turns the story around is her taking David and running. Once she runs, the change of direction in the story is inevitable. What moves the second act into third-act resolution is not the DSS going to court to institutionalise David, it is Sally coming back and confronting them. Until she does that, they cannot proceed with their action.

Could the turning points be different within the story contexts we examined in Chapter 2? Yes. If Sally was seen to be totally vulnerable, a victim in the set-up, then you could structure the first-act turning point as that moment when she does an about-face and takes control. This would depend on where you were 'pitching' your story, and what kind of dramatic dynamics you were aiming for. It's possible, though, to use a change in a character's attitude—that moment when the character consciously chooses to dictate the action rather than be a victim of it—as a turning point.

A writer friend of mine describes the turning point as the moment in the script without which there would be no story. That is certainly true up to a point, although you would still have a story. It just wouldn't be the story you set out to tell.

Exercises

1   If you have a written screenplay, go to it now and identify your first-act turning point. Now do the same with your second. If you can't identify them immediately, make a note of what and where you think they are, so that you can come back to them at the end of this chapter.

2   Write out your story in four pages . . . not three or five, *four*. You will find that you eliminate all extraneous development and stick to your plot. Now look for your first-act turning point. It should be somewhere around one-third of the way down page two. You'll find that it ends a paragraph, or is a complete paragraph on its own. Identify your second-act turning point. You should find it close to the top of page four. Again, it will close off a paragraph, and the beginning of your new paragraph will be the opening of act three. If you can't find turning points at all, circle the areas on the page and look at what's happening to your storyline at that point. Now, put this exercise on hold, but repeat it after each

of the following three sections, when you know more about your structure.

Let's now look at the acts themselves and examine the function of each.

Act one—the beginning

Every film starts its story with an image, and then links that image to a person. There may well be dialogue, or music score, but it's what you are seeing, rather than what you are hearing, that determines your initial interest. Sometimes the first image will seem to have nothing to do with the story that follows but, if you saw the film a second time, you would realise that the image helped create a mood, a feeling, and that in turn prepared you for the story you have to take on board as the film unfolds.

This is the beginning of your set-up. Act one does not consist entirely of a set-up, but the set-up is of utmost importance to the audience.

Assuming that your script is of average length (around 100 pages), your first act will run (roughly) from pages 1–25, and your set-up will cover the first 10–15 pages. By the end of those pages you will need to have conveyed to the audience the following information:

Who your main characters are
What they do and why (you will keep expanding on this)
What the style is
What the genre is
What the story's about
Where it's set

Once the audience understands these things, they stop simply being observers and asking those questions, and they become participants. In the next 10–15 pages a new question emerges for the audience and they will start asking, 'What's going to happen?' By now they know that the film's about a girl from the country who has a handicapped child; who has an illness; who's in need of help; who's living in the city and so on and so on . . . and they've reached the end of the set-up. They identify (one hopes) with Sally and her predicament. Now you have roughly ten pages to introduce action, people actually doing something which in turn leads to an event which will push both character and audience into the first-act turning point. In our 'Sally and Son' story the action starts when Sally determines to find someone to look after David. Everything up to that point where the doctor tells her the truth is set-up. Once she initiates action she starts a chain of events which inevitably leads to potential danger for herself and David.

It is the fact of the DSS investigating Sally which leads to her developing her fear of losing David and causes her to run. This kind of event is usually referred to as the springboard or the *catalyst*, and it always appears to be a major plot point, the question one asks about the film. For, although Sally runs and we are catapulted into new adventures in the second act, the question has been set up for us by the catalyst. That is, 'Will the DSS take Sally's son?'

Now, if we look back at that first act we will see, only a quarter of the way through the film, that we've introduced character, predicament, and raised the central question. Our audience has a firm hook on the story we're telling and should not be confused about anything. They know the style and genre, and they know what they're going to get. But they don't know how they're going to get it.

Act one usually conveys more information to the audience than the rest of your script put together. It's the old journalistic, 'Who, what, where, when, why?' encapsulated. Because it contains so much information, it plays at a slower rate, and in a lower gear, than the other two acts. This isn't accidental. It is vital if you want the audience to assimilate all you have to tell them. If you hit them with one adrenalin rush after another at the same time as you're trying to convey important character information, they'll never keep up.

Of course, action movies are an exception, because their driving force is the adrenalin rush and as long as they keep it pumping there's little concern about whether the audience relates to the characters or is asking the central question. Even so, it's fair to say that action movies do contain a set-up that plays at a much slower rate than the rest of the film. It's just that the set-up is generally shorter and the central question is normally, 'Who is going to get killed', the answer to which may well start to be revealed in the first-act turning point.

Exercise

Repeat the last exercise (see p. 62). Is your set-up in the right place? Does your first-act turning point come where the audience will expect it? Have you raised the central question in your story? If not, rewrite your four pages.

Act two—the middle

Act two forms the bulk of your script, more than half its running
time. This could mean between 45–60 minutes of screen time.
Moreover, you have to create conflict and confrontation, keep
the story moving forward and stop the audience from losing
interest. Most screenplays get through their first act reasonably
well. Structural problems seem always to occur in the second
act. How often have you heard someone say, 'I fell asleep halfway
through'. Or perhaps you have even done it yourself.

So, how do we hold the audience's attention for this length
of time? What, in our Sally story, is the basis for our second
act? Sally goes on the run with David. The DSS try to track her
down. Terrific. Two facts that need to be expanded to nearly an
hour of screen time and generate interest. Piece of cake. There
are no limitations on us as to *how* Sally keeps ahead of the DSS
or *what* happens to her. We have open slather on creating
conflict, confrontation, stumbling blocks, crises and so forth. We
can introduce incidents that stand on their own as mini-stories
or short-form subplots played over perhaps as few as 4–6 scenes,
or as many as twenty. The point is that the mini-story is
generally told as a whole. These are called *plot sequences* (as
opposed to a subplot which may run over your entire three-act
script) and we will examine them shortly. The one thing vital to
keeping this second act afloat is momentum.

Momentum

We've all heard the word, but what does it mean? It means the
constantly accelerating rate at which your story keeps moving
forward towards its conclusion. Again, as with most things other
than your initial brilliant idea, it is not an art form, it is a craft
skill, and it is not accidental. To achieve momentum is simple
in theory, but difficult in practice. It requires a strong connection
between the scenes and a constant progression in plot and
character development. In Chapter 11 I will give some practical
demonstrations of recognising how and where you lost it, but
for now let's understand the principle and the practical application. So, what we're looking for is a natural relationship between
scenes so that what happens in one scene is the direct springboard to the development of the next scene, which in turn is
strongly connected to the scene that follows.

It's similar to the causal relationship discussed in Chapter 4,
and is part of the action/interaction/ reaction equation. This

doesn't mean that every scene has a story or plot point in it. But it does mean that we don't lose sight of the story, the conflict, that they are kept alive either through the characters' attitudes or in the underlying tension of the scene. So an action in one scene leads to a reaction, which generates another action in the next scene, and so on and so forth. Momentum, in my opinion, is always in the hands of the characters. It is they who must keep the story moving forward even if there are no new developments in the plot.

Thrust, impulsion, pace

You will probably have heard of the third but may not be familiar with the first two. If you are asked, 'What's the thrust of the story?' you are actually being asked: what's driving it, what creates the drama, where is the sense of urgency coming from, what's behind the conflict, where is the threat? (Now you know why it's easier to ask about the thrust.) Our story is about a young single mother going on the run to keep her child. But that is not what is controlling the dynamic range of the story in dramatic terms. No. These are created by the thrust, which in turn can be identified as the spectre of the DSS, looming always just behind Sally, ready to grab her child and devour it. We've said that in order to maintain momentum the relationship between the scenes must be constantly moving forward to unfold the story. This means that Sally must be constantly moving forward. What keeps her moving forward? The sense of urgency: if she lets her guard down and the DSS finds her, it will take her son. Without the DSS, she'd have no reason to run. The thrust is not the same as the focus of the script. The focus is where our attention is held, the view that we follow. Sally's actual dilemma and how she deals with it is the focus. It is that element behind the focus that compels the script (as well as the character) to move forward. That's the thrust.

Impulsion is a name I give to something which many writers think is part of momentum, and others believe is simply instinct. Certainly it's like trying to pin a tangible label on something that is quite abstract. I define it as the pulse, or breathing rate, of your script; the life force that keeps it moving. If you want your script to represent a living identifiable world, then it has to breathe. In music, impulsion would be the rate at which the metronome determines the tempo. That ticking of a metronome, or the tapping of your foot, is constant whether you're playing slow or fast notes in the melody line. Your script will have its own breathing rate, its own pulse, its own tempo (the underlying speed at which it plays, as opposed to the changes in rhythm, or the long and short notes of the melody which are superimposed over it). The interesting thing about this very abstract concept is that one can see physical manifestations in the reactions of an audience. This is quite separate from your plot, your genre and the momentum you create. Once the audience takes on board the breathing rate or tempo of your script, it adjusts accordingly and makes that tempo its own. This is why a seemingly slow movie in which nothing much seems to happen can be absolutely spellbinding. Firstly, the momentum has been maintained through all three acts and, secondly, the audience has adapted to the impulsion or tempo of the script. It's breathing long deep breaths which fill its lungs, rather than short panting ones. Isn't this related to the pace, you may be asking? (I once spent a whole day trying to explain the differences to an inexperienced writer before giving up in frustration.) No, the two are entirely different.

Pace is a peculiar animal that is often wrongly handled. It is a visible creature whilst thrust and impulsion are invisible. Pace is the speed at which things happen within the framework of a scene or a sequence. It's a marvellous thing if it finds its own level, accelerating in direct relationship to the rate at which the story unfolds, and is not artificially imposed. Unfortunately it is often injected in the form of visual action, to provide a quick adrenalin burst for the audience, into a script that has lost momentum and a story which has ground to a halt. It will not restore momentum, and it's quite likely to halt impulsion too.

Often it comes in the form of a car chase, a helicopter flight with a big explosion, or a huge physical fight. Mostly it happens when the actual unfolding of the story has reached an impasse. But once this action sequence has finished, your script is back in the same rut. You still have to propel your story forward and restore momentum. All you've done is sidetrack the audience for a few minutes. If, on the other hand, your action sequence actually contains vital information for advancing the storyline, then you will find that the momentum is automatically restored. The problem you face then is that the pace can mean that things move at a frenetic speed, much faster than the audience is used to. Since they have already adjusted to the impulsion of the script, they're going to have to work doubly hard to keep up with you. Any plot points hurried through in the momentum are liable to be lost on them and it all becomes too hard.

Mentally they switch off, even though their eyes are still engaged.
Mostly they'll react later to the loss of concentration by saying,
'The plot was too complicated, it lost me.' The plot probably
wasn't too complicated at all—very few films are that complicated. More likely the plot points were just introduced too fast,
in the effort to create pace, for the audience to take them all on
board. Thus vital information was missed, the story stopped
making sense, the film lost its audience. Pace is essential for all
scripts, but it needs to be an integral part of the storytelling
process and, when it is, it then links directly with momentum.
Some genres require more pace than others. Comedies require
action that generates laughs, that is, pace. Thrillers require
action that generates tension and fear, that is, pace.

Plot sequences

Earlier in this chapter I mentioned the business of creating
material for the second act through self-contained short-form
mini-stories called plot sequences. The key word here is *plot*.
There are no restrictions as to what constitutes content for these
creatures, provided that the word plot is seen to be integral to
the sequence. This means that it should have an implicit relationship to the main story, the central question, and the thrust
of the script. If it doesn't, it means you're going off on a tangent
and losing the direction of your script. That inevitably involves
a loss of momentum. Let's create two of these mini-stories for
'Sally and Son' and see why one works and the other doesn't.

a) Sally arrives in a strange town. Unable to draw welfare
money she answers an ad for a babysitter and meets Karen,
who has three kids under five and has just gone back to
part-time teaching. Karen takes a shine to Sally and gives
her the job. David gets on really well with the three kids and
Sally sees first-hand what it's like to have a real home and
family. But making ends meet on child-minding wages is
nigh-on impossible and Karen can see that Sally is going
without food. Karen is married to Jack, a terrific husband
and father who loves the way his wife jumps in to help what
he calls 'lame ducks'. He meets Sally and David, and wonders
why she isn't drawing welfare, which would at least give her
a health card and concessions to make life a little easier.
Sally is evasive. Unbeknown to her, Jack is a social worker,
attached to the family court in the strange town. Sally has
inadvertently let drop the name of the town where she comes
from. Jack, in a genuine attempt to help her get support,

does some checking on the computer as he tries to get info from the DSS in Sally's home town. Lo and behold, he punches up details about a young woman with a handicapped child . . . Sally and David. He makes a couple of calls, discovers the true story and now is in a dilemma. He confides in Karen. Sally is sick, she needs medical help, DSS are only trying to make things easy for her. Karen doesn't agree. She figures that if Sally, who she has gleaned is not stupid, chose to run, she had legitimate fears. Jack struggles with his conscience and decides to notify the DSS. But Karen pre-empts him. She warns Sally, gives her extra money and some clothes and the two part, knowing they will never see each other again.

b) Sally, as before, arrives in the strange town. A gang of young hoons in a beat-up car terrorises her while she is shopping. A 'white knight' arrives on a Harley, hauls Sally up behind him, and gives chase. The hoons get away. Sally is attracted to the man—let's call him Jake. There's an air of danger about him that she's never encountered before. He's with a local touring carnival and he invites Sally and David there for the day. David is ecstatic, wanting to go on every ride, and there's clearly a lot of lust building up between Sally and Jake. While Sally and David are on the Ferris wheel, the gears snap in the motor and it goes out of control. It spins wildly until Jake is able to smash the motor and jam the cogs. Now Sally and David are stuck sixty feet up in the air and David is hysterical, flailing about wildly, liable to fall. Jake climbs the scaffolding with the agility of a mountaineer, rescues mother and child and carries them back down, using his belt to strap David to him. He spends that night with Sally, but the following day the carnival moves on, and Sally is left with only a memory of the excitement she experienced.

Which story do you prefer? Which story maintains the momentum? Which adds the most pace? Which belongs in the script?

Story a) belongs in the script, story b) doesn't. If you look at the rules you will see that story b) adds a great deal of superficial pace, but halts the script in its tracks. Although Sally is a major player in the story, there is no link between this story and our plot, nor is there any connection to our central question. What story b) does is put all momentum on hold, suspends any forward movement of the script, and sidetracks the audience into another area which does not advance even the major characters. It might be great fun. It would probably provide terrific visuals, but it's got nothing to do with the script and, much as you might love the whole feel of it, it would have to go in order to save the script from serious illness.

Story a), on the other hand, while being totally self-contained, actually adds to the momentum. Why? Because it not only keeps the story moving forward in the direction that was intended, it reinforces the threat to Sally and enhances the sense of urgency, thus creating its very own, real, pace. It doesn't matter that we never meet Karen or Jack again. Their actions, and interaction with Sally, lead directly to a reaction which compels the story to move forward again.

Put another way, if your script is a highway leading to a specific destination, then story a) is a detour which is still part of the journey. Story b), on the other hand, is a diversion which leads to a dead end, and you would have to turn around and backtrack all the way to the point where you left the highway.

You may see these plot sequences referred to or identified as vignettes, but that's really a misnomer. Vignettes are those charming moments in films which take the characters (and audience) out of themselves for a brief while. But they generally do not contain their own three-act structure, and are usually unresolved. They may put the story on hold momentarily, but they usually don't take us in entirely the wrong direction. In terms of our highway metaphor they are, perhaps, roundabouts. We pause, swing round in a circle, then simply move on.

You can see how easy it is for a writer to get off the track in that second act, can't you? And there really is no excuse. All that's needed is to remember what your destination is in story terms and to stay on the main route, even if you have to stop to refuel along the way.

Act three—the end

Resolution is the key word here, and that does of course mean providing an ending for our script, but that isn't all this act is about. It's about closure, tying up loose ends, indicating whether or not your main character got what he/she wanted/needed. You'll notice that I said *providing an ending for our script*, rather than an end for the character's story. Sally's story doesn't end when she beats the DSS, gets to keep David as well as receiving help from the courts. That's only where the script ends. The character still has to deal with her illness, get off welfare, get educated, find a job, get a life, etc. Her story is her life; we've just been writing (or viewing) a small part of it.

The act-two turning point throws us inexorably into act three. The audience can generally see what's coming now; the climax looms ahead of them. Mostly they can pick the outcome, but that doesn't matter.

When we reach this turning point in act two we're once again confronted early in the third act with the central question, reminded of it by the decision or choice which inevitably faces the main character. It's also often the moment when the main character stops running away and starts running towards. Thus we change direction again, this time a complete reversal. It is the moment when, if he/she hasn't already done so, the main character takes control and aggressively pursues the resolution instead of acting defensively.

Since act three usually consists of the lead character initiating the climax (either by attacking or facing what is most feared), it's logical that this act will once again change gear, gather momentum, use more thrust, increase impulsion, and pick up real pace. Because the end is in sight, and because there can only be one winner in a conflict, there is also more at stake. There are no longer any second chances, any strategies to be pursued—this is a head-on clash. Do or die! It's that moment—whether we're talking about a Hollywood action film or a gentle human-interest drama. Sometimes the ending is bleak, and the main character loses. That's fine if we have been expecting that loss all along. More often than not the victim becomes the winner and we all cheer, because that's what we'd been hoping for all along.

In 'Sally and Son', the act two turning point is where she digs her heels in and says, 'No more. These bastards aren't going to keep me running for the rest of my life.'

In act three she returns and confronts the DSS, telling them she will fight them in court. Now we're heading for the showdown, the climax and our central question is raised and kept in front of us. Will the DSS succeed in taking David? Our actual climax will come probably five pages or so before the end. This will be where Sally triumphs. It might be an impassioned speech to the judge. There could be a twist; perhaps she's been studying law in night school and she's found a statute she can use . . . maybe she's enlisted the help of the media to press her case. At any rate it will satisfy the audience without being too predictable. They can guess what the outcome will be, but they shouldn't be forewarned of the actual mechanics. Our final few pages, the resolution, will tie up the loose ends, promise better days ahead, answer any questions we've left dangling from the previous two acts. Some films don't even go that far. In Alfred Hitchcock's *North by Northwest* (MGM 1959), the climax comes as Eva Marie Saint dangles precariously from Mount Rushmore and Cary Grant reaches out his hand. Jump-cut to the upper berth of a sleeping compartment on a train as he pulls her, now his wife, up beside him. Climax followed by a fifteen-second resolution. That's one extreme, but the opposite is more often true. A film will often take too long to resolve, we'll still be tying up loose ends fifteen minutes after the climax. Tie loose ends up before the climax if you have so many. Leave only those that are in doubt until the climax decides them one way or the other. Whatever type of story you are telling, your climax is going to be your point of maximum dramatic impact. Spending too long on your resolution not only diffuses that impact, it gives the audience a false sense that maybe the story isn't over after all. They then wait for an even bigger climax, and are disappointed when it doesn't happen.

So, with any luck, we now have a good grounding in three-act structure. We know not only what needs to be done, but when and how to do it. Before we go off to celebrate I have to point out that we've only broken down our main story. We have yet to tackle that other demon, the subplot.

2 SUBPLOTS—THE LIMBS

Your subplot is a secondary storyline. It may be one of many. It is integral to the story you are telling, but it does not carry as much weight in terms of action. It may well run from the first act of your script through to the third act, or it may be resolved far earlier. The point is that it intersects your main storyline at any number of given points (either physically or cerebrally), and it will involve at least one of the characters who is also responsible for creating action in your main story (it may even be the two main characters). So how do you determine whether your subplot is a secondary storyline or merely an expansion of your main, linear storyline? You take your storyline back to the basic premise and then swiftly develop it without your subplot. Can you still tell your story? If you can't, then what you've cut may not be subplot. But my bet is that you can.

Most writers reach a stage when they're 'pitching' an idea where the subplot, no matter how large, is never mentioned.

Does this make subplots superfluous? Not at all. Very often it's the subplot that provides the audience with that psychological profile we talked about in character creation. While your main storyline must always be about 'doing', your subplot is most often about 'being'. It's also a useful way of conveying your underlying theme to the audience, the 'message' of your script, if you like. In 'Sally and Son' the issues we would want to raise are about welfare dependency, loneliness, fear of bureaucracy, emotional alienation. They're not issues that are answered in our storyline, whose central question is 'Will the DSS take David?' That's a tangible process denoted by action. Our subplot, however, can pose any number of philosophical questions which may be answered by character growth rather than character action. Of course, we'd expect to see a change in action because of that growth. So our subplot would then directly intersect our main storyline.

Subplots are often concerned with the love story in a film script. This is logical, since it's usually when a person commits to another that they really start to look at themselves and make changes. In 'Sally and Son' we know that Sally comes back to face the DSS. It's most likely that the subplot provides the motivation for that decision. (Remember, we're still in social-issue drama mode.) It could well be a man/woman love story that gives her strength and also gives us, as the writers, the chance to explore some of the concepts behind the main story-line: Sally's fear; her isolation; her need to be free of the system, and so on.

But what if it were a sisterhood love that examined the questions we need answered about Sally, through looking at a secondary character? Something like this:

Sally meets Annie, another single mother, who has two kids, 4-year-old Skye and 3-year-old Brooke. Annie is bright and funny and is a junkie who has been clean since Brooke's birth. Annie milks the system for all its worth, and has no desire to get off it, which shocks Sally who is at the same time impressed by Annie's attitude. For Annie seems afraid of nothing, she just goes with the flow and enjoys every day. Annie loves her kids, but doesn't take parenting very seriously. Often she'll leave them alone at night while she goes out. She and Sally become good friends, and each has a profound effect on the other. She clarifies Sally's ideas, by her actions and attitudes, about a very different life she wants for herself and David. Brooke dies in an accident while Annie is out at the pub one night. Annie, full of remorse and guilt, cracks up and turns back to drugs. She's hauled into court after being arrested, and the court takes Skye away from her. Annie kills herself.

We can see immediately how the Annie subplot can carry the message, raise the philosophical arguments and instigate character growth in Sally. Yet, although it enforces our main storyline, our script can play without it, and it is not what we would talk about in telling our story in fifty words or less.

The other interesting thing we can see is that this subplot has its own three-act structure. The set-up is very clear, the first turning point comes when Brooke dies, the second when Annie is hauled into court on drug charges. We know that the climax will be that Skye is taken away. It's inevitable, and the resolution is Annie killing herself. This downbeat ending in the subplot serves to reinforce the upbeat ending in the main storyline. The turning points in the subplot may also help initiate the turning points in the main story. For example, Annie's suicide strengthens Sally's resolve to control her own life and is the catalyst for the turning point of her going back to face the issues confronting her.

Your script may carry as many as four or five subplots of differing importance. Each will in some way convey to the audience more information about what's happening to the central characters or the underlying theme itself. Each will have its own three-act structure, and its own character development.

7

Adapting the structure

TV DRAMA—THE MANY-HEADED HYBRID

What happens to the three-act structure if we are writing our script for commercial television? (We can safely assume that the three-act structure, perhaps with a shortened set-up, remains intact for ABC formats.) If there are five commercial breaks and six segments, as there are in any one hour of Australian television drama (overseas productions tend to have four segments in an hour), don't we have six acts and five turning points? The answer is yes—and no.

Inescapably, all stories have beginnings, middles and ends. What you are imposing on that structure, or adding to it, might be called the middle of the beginning, the middle of the middle, the middle of the end. These 'middles' are plot points which are enlarged to leave an element of doubt about the outcome. They don't turn the plot around as a turning point does, but they pose the question, 'Is the plot going to turn around?' and they form the basis for the commercial break. So we may have a scene at the end of a segment where someone is holding a gun on a major character and the fear is that they will shoot. Cut to the commercial break. But of course we know, as writers and audience members, that this major character is not going to get killed. The programme is less than half the way through, and the hero/heroine is going to be there at the end.

So the question is not, 'Will the main character be killed?' but rather, 'Might the main character be injured?' which is a question the audience doesn't know the answer to. More often

75

than not, the answer is provided within one or two scenes after the commercials. The antagonist is disarmed, and the character moves on with the story. If there were no commercial break and the two scenes became one, this plot point would probably constitute no more than a moment of action within the context of the script. Instead, what has happened is that the scene leading into the commercial break has created artificial tension, or anxiety, in the mind of the viewer which lasts at least the duration of the commercial break. In other words, we have suspended the action in a given plot point, to allow for the insertion of a three-minute break, without suspending the audience interest, thus ensuring that they will keep watching.

Sometimes we will not know whether the 'out' to the commercial break is simply a tease or a genuine turning point, and that, too, keeps us viewing. For example, if we came back after the commercial break and discovered that the gunman was a kidnapper who takes our main character for a terrifying journey, which is in fact what our story is about, then the earlier scene would have been the act one turning point and we'd now be in act two. It's this intriguing uncertainty that determines the dynamics of television drama.

The new writer might glean from this that the six-segment drama would break down as follows:

Turning points = second and fourth commercial breaks.
Middle points (enhanced plot points or suspended action) = first, third and fifth commercial breaks, thus making the second and fourth commercial breaks the most important.

Not so. It might seem logical in a structural sense, but when one balances dynamics with demographics and commercial revenue, one gets a completely different equation. In the six-segment drama, the most important breaks are the first and third, with the fifth generally constructed around the climax, so that the sixth segment comprises the resolution. The first and sixth segments are almost always the shortest (though this may not be so in serials), leaving little time for a set-up before a major dramatic moment leads into the first commercial break.

Let's look at why this happens.

The various networks in Australia start each programming segment at roughly the same time. The viewer makes a choice about what to watch. The opening credits plus the set-up will run 5–6 minutes. If the viewer is not hooked by the first commercial break, it is not too late to change channels and pick up some other programme. So there is often a foreshortened set-up which leads to either a very strong plot point or a turning point occurring at the first commercial break. When the viewer returns for the second segment, there may be a resumption of the first-act set-up and introduction of characters.

Sometimes the first segment doesn't contain a set-up at all, or a first-act turning point. Sometimes it is an entirely separate entity, a teaser which will only lead us into the main story after the commercial break, much like the prologue of a book, or the pre-credit sequence of some films. Whatever, the chief purpose of that first segment is to hook the audience and hold it across the commercial break into the second segment.

On the other hand, by the time we get to the second break, the programme on the other channel will be roughly 16–18 minutes old. If we change now there's a good chance that we won't be able to pick up the story, especially since the programme on the other channel will have employed exactly the same tactics. So, more often than not, our second and third segments constitute our first act, with the second commercial break creating artificial intrigue, and the third commercial break being a turning point. Or it may be the other way round, but in that case the third break would then need to be enhanced even more strongly to sustain the interest.

Why is the third commercial break so important?

Because as I mentioned earlier, an opposing network may have its programming for that night in half-hour format. Therefore, if you're bored by the time you reach the third commercial break, you could still turn over and catch the beginning of a half-hour sitcom or similar. The fourth commercial break is usually the catalyst for the second-act turning point, so naturally the viewer will stay with it to find out what's going to happen. That second-act turning point will usually happen early in the fifth segment, with the climax forming the fifth commercial break. The final segment is the resolution.

We can still clearly see a three-act structure, even though the lengths of the acts may be very different to the paradigm for film, and may well vary from programme to programme. This would hold for any six-part one-hour drama with a self-contained story element. In a mini-series our first-act turning point may not happen until near the end of the first hour (which would be halfway through the first episode). Thus we would have had four or five commercial breaks requiring the construction of 'highs' in plot point terms, or a suspension of action to create intrigue across a break.

The sitcom is a two-segment creature in Britain and the

United States, but a three-segment format here in Australia, and so it's obviously easier to see how the three-act structure breaks down. The same can be said of children's drama, usually in half-hour format.

The television serial, however, whether it's in a one-hour six-segment format, or half-hour three-segment (I've noticed lately some four-segment half-hours), defies the rules to the extent that it doesn't generally carry a major storyline through a three-act structure at all. What it does instead is balance a number of subplots which will run over a given number of weeks (often not decided at the time of creating the story). We call this open-ended storytelling. Each story will have its three-act structure, but it will be almost impossible to determine where the acts turned, as this may occur over a number of episodes, or even weeks or months. Moreover, because the content is about a group of people, or a collection of happenings, the only time everything gets resolved is in the final episode after the serial has been axed!

Of course, individual stories are resolved. However, that resolution rarely forms the end of an episode, although it will most likely be the penultimate scene. The last scene of any serial episode is the cliffhanger. The name implies precisely the meaning—a moment of action or dramatic conflict set up to leave the audience hanging in suspense until the following episode, where it is always resolved within the first segment, and most often in the first scene. So the storyline that formed your cliffhanger in one episode will most likely dominate the first segment of the next episode, even if it is fully resolved before the end of that episode.

You can see that in a half-hour serial, which constitutes only 22 minutes of actual script time (and this includes opening and end credits and the recap of the last cliffhanger) and balances as many as four storylines at a given time, there is little time for nuance or subtlety. Let's look at an example of a three-segment set-up and see how the separate storylines might dominate each segment. We'll letter them A–B–C, and their order in the segments denotes their prominence.

Pre-credit	Seg. 1	Seg. 2	Seg. 3
A	A	B	B
B	B	C	C
	C		A

What we'd glean from this is that the A storyline carried the last episode cliffhanger, but since it's actually a story which is winding down, or perhaps being put on hold (rested) for a few episodes, it may even miss a segment. The B storyline has been backing up the A storyline, but now it's taking over. It forms the cliffhanger for this episode and therefore will figure strongly in the first segment of the following episode. The C storyline figures in only one scene in the first segment. Perhaps it's a brand new storyline, one that needs to be introduced and built quickly. Once established, it eases off to allow the B storyline to dominate the final segment.

Even looking at this primitive example, you can see that structuring serials is more difficult than you might have thought. However, it's seldom that you would need to be so specific with a given episode. Serials are created in blocks, generally of five episodes per block, and it's of much greater importance how your stories balance over the week. So your chart might, hypothetically, look more like this:

Ep. 1	Ep. 2	Ep. 3	Ep. 4	Ep. 5
B	B	C	C	B
A	C	B	D	C
C	A	D	B	D

Within this one block, one week's screenings, we have finished story A, introduced story D, built story B to a point where it will be the focal point at week's end, and established story C as the major candidate to carry the following block.

In reality, far more storylines are usually involved in the juggling act. In *Arcade* we had 27 characters and as many as nine storylines. These were juggled over five episodes a week of 22 minutes running time each. It's not hard to understand why the programme never found an audience. *Prisoner* was a one-hour show, twice a week. Over that two-hour block we would normally run five storylines.

Of course, once you break your episode down into scenes (probably anywhere from 17–25 in an episode) it becomes easier to juggle the storylines. This is done by 'looping'. So storyline A might appear in scenes 1, 3, 5, and storyline B would form scenes 2, 4, and so on. If we expanded on the small chart above, we might have something like this:

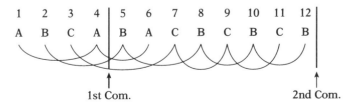

We'd be two-thirds of the way through an episode and we would have rested the A storyline in order to build B and push C.

Keeping track of the three-act structure in serial television is a nightmare, even though every story does have a beginning, a middle and an end. Momentum is not created in the normal way either, because one scene rarely links with another in the same storyline, being broken up by scenes from other storylines. Rather it is manufactured from the juxtaposition of storylines and (in good soap) from within the scenes themselves. First and foremost in building momentum in serials is the maintaining of the question in the audience's mind, 'What's going to happen next?'

I mentioned in my very first chapter that one medium was not necessarily more difficult to write for than the other, but that they required different skills. I hope it is easier now to see why. More than skills, though, is the approach or attitude required—a difference of visual exploration for film as opposed to frenetic energy for television, and there's room in writing for both.

8

Dialogue and scene construction

WHO SAID WHAT TO WHOM—AND WHERE?

Normally you would expect these two subjects to occupy different chapters in a book (if you found them at all). I've grouped them together because, firstly, they are interdependent and, secondly, they fulfill the same function within a screenplay, whether it be for film or television.

That function can be broken down into a number of elements, which then allow us to judge whether our dialogue and our scenes are doing the job they were meant to. So we can say that, either alone or in combination, and in no particular order, dialogue and scene construction:

- create an action/interaction/reaction equation which constitutes the storytelling process;
- convey new information to the audience;
- advance the plot, or storyline;
- advance the character development;
- create conflict and tension;
- carry the audience forward on a journey;
- move the audience and/or the characters physically through time and location;
- convey moods and attitudes;
- delineate changes to either of the above;
- open up ideas and philosophies, often subliminally.

Of course, not every scene, or dialogue exchange, does all those things. But if you have a scene, containing dialogue, which does

81

none of those things, no matter how interesting the location, or how witty the banter, it is not a scene.

Dialogue

By its very definition, dialogue is verbal communication between two or more people. The person who initiates the dialogue performs an action. The person who responds performs a reaction—between the two we have an interaction. So, there's no doubt that our equation is a constantly recurring process in screenwriting.

It shouldn't be that hard to have people talk to each other, express ideas and convey information which move the story forward. Yet dialogue is one of the banes of the writer's life. Often stilted and stultifyingly boring, it can slow a script with great story momentum to a standstill. Mostly this happens when characters exchange monologues, talking *at* each other rather than with each other. Sometimes these monologues are full of dreadful exposition (more about that later). Sometimes the characters have nothing to say and the dialogue has been artificially imposed without subtext (more about that later too.) Most often the problem is that the writer simply hasn't found the right voice for the character.

Finding the voice

What does it mean, to find the right voice for a character? It means taking on board all that you know about your character and, from that, deducing speech patterns which could legitimately belong to that person.

This means not only examining the socio-economic status of the character, but the personality as well. Characters who are shy, or maybe introverted, aren't going to make great long articulate speeches. Their eloquence, if they have it at all, is going to have to come from what they *don't* say—witness Sylvester Stallone in *Rocky*. A poorly educated person is not going to use three-syllable (or more) words, or obscure language, unless that person has delusions of grandeur and uses the words incorrectly without knowing the true meaning. Characters with low self-esteem are going to find it hard to express themselves at all, so their speech will often be disjointed and halting. We have all seen actors whose dialogue appears to be a series of grunts and half-uttered words. We applaud the actor for the characterisation, the 'method' acting, and forget entirely that a writer wrote, or should have written, it that way in the first place.

Many writers, though, tend to write dialogue as though they never intend it to be said aloud. I don't write the way I speak. I know of very few people who do. Yet I see dozens of screenplays where all the characters have exactly the same speech patterns. The dialogue may read well on the page, but the minute you speak it out loud it's laughable, often consisting of people pontificating to the audience rather than communicating with each other. Remember: *the characters don't know they are in a film*, etc, etc.

It's essential first to find the voice. Supposing your character is just an average, reasonably adjusted, middle-class person? It makes no difference. We all have idiosyncracies, pet words or phrases, speech rhythms and habits. We talk fast, or slow, leave sentences unfinished. I am told that my pet word at the moment is 'bizarre' and that I drop it in at every opening. I'm not aware of doing so, it's just a quirk. I also tend to talk quickly and impatiently. Your characters won't all express themselves the same way, and none of them should be expressing themselves like you, the writer. Once you've found the voice for your character, it should be possible to cover over the characters' names by the halfway mark of your script and still have the reader know exactly who is speaking at any given time.

When you reach that stage, it's imperative that you say your dialogue out loud, preferably with a few friends to play other characters. You'll instantly find places where the tongue just won't follow the speech; where the reader trips over sentences or starts paraphrasing. Writers often decry the fact that actors rewrite their dialogue, but quite often the truth is that the dialogue is literally unspeakable. We write on paper, but our work is not designed to be read. It is meant to be heard and seen. The only way to know whether it works or not is to actually hear and see it before you impose it on someone else. I know of many diabolical films where the producer has told me, 'It read well on the page'.

As an actor I've been forced to stamp my foot occasionally. Here's an example of two pieces of dialogue (to the best of my memory) from consecutive episodes of the soap in which I played Consuela, the fat receptionist at the gym. In the first I storm into the coffee shop, plonk myself down at the table and say something like:

'Good arvo Robbie. Jeez, I'm starvin'! Gimme a bite of yer sanger, will ya?'

One episode later I sit at a desk looking pensive and say: 'I'm not too certain of the legal technicalities, but I feel certain that the child, once it is born, would be entitled to a goodly portion of its father's estate.'

A goodly portion? Give me a break! Yet this script went past an editor, a script typist, the producer, production manager, director (and probably their families) before the poor hapless actor (me) had to say it out loud.

Finding the voice for the individual character isn't all that's involved in creating workable dialogue. Another set of values comes into play depending upon the relationship of the characters interacting in the dialogue. Are they speaking differently from their normal speech patterns because they're trying to impress each other? Do they share a mutual attitude, so that dialogue is compatible, or is there conflict in the interaction because of differing moods? Dialogue is communication, we all agree. But what about when one person is hearing something different to what the other is saying?

And do all people communicate the same way?

Here is something that you learn with age, rather than from writing experience. The better two people know each other, the longer they have been together, the less they have to say to each other. One of my favourite screenplays of all time is Frederick Raphael's *Two for the Road* (20th Century Fox/Stanley Donen Prods 1967). In it, Audrey Hepburn and Albert Finney go through all the stages of a marriage breaking down, but the sequences don't play in chronological order. At one stage, when they first fall in love (she wants the ring, he doesn't), they watch a couple eat dinner without exchanging a word. She asks, 'What kind of people have nothing to say to each other?' He answers 'Married people'. Two lines that are full of subtext and ask and answer a dozen questions about the different ways in which each is approaching the relationship. Later on in life she echoes his response as they sit silently at dinner. Beautiful writing. In this context, his response has negative connotations. In reality, of course, the fact that two characters who've known each other for a long time don't talk can have diametrically opposed explanations.

a) They don't talk because they've said everything there is to say; they're bored with each other; the relationship is stale— *negative*.

b) They don't talk because speech is superfluous; they communicate on a much deeper level; they know what each other is thinking; they anticipate every thought; they're bonded together so deeply that it's as if they share a secret—*positive*.

One action, but two reactions, and totally different interaction. It follows our either/or framework in character construction (see Chapter 5). The negative relationship is far easier to write about than the positive, and both rely heavily on attitude, mood and body language to convey the right signals. Both are also simple examples of subtext working at its most manageable level, and we'll examine that in the next chapter.

The approach to dialogue in film is to cut as much of it as possible and replace it with visual interaction. Otherwise your screenplay ends up as what is termed derogatively (try saying that word out loud in dialogue) 'talking heads'. The opposite is often true in television. Here, no chances are taken that the audience may lose important information by turning away from the screen for a moment. So everything tends to be verbalised, just to make sure, and visuals, apart from supplying backdrops for action, tend to mirror moods or emotions which have already been conveyed through language.

Exposition

This is the transference, through dialogue, from one character to another, and thus to the audience, of essential information. In television, exposition is accepted as a necessary evil, for there simply isn't the time, or the dynamic range, to 'bleed' information in slowly and subtly. Remember we talked about cliffhangers in serials? Often a cliffhanger will be exposition, the blatant disclosure of someone's past, or hidden secret.

In film, this kind of exposition would be an aberration. It's clumsy and heavy-handed, and seems more so because it's on a big screen. There are ways of handling exposition in subtext and I'll give practical examples in the next chapter. Obviously there will always be information that characters have to convey to each other, and there will be important points to be made for the audience's benefit. If it is general information, it is better to filter it in over a number of scenes, a little at a time. If it is a major revelation, then of course it can be the moment of dramatic impact in a scene.

Too often exposition is simply stating the obvious. Most problematical is when the characters say things that they would never actually say, simply in order to convey information to an audience. People do not constantly talk in detail about things they already know and have discussed at great length. Certain things are understood between them. Certain subjects are taboo.

Let's look at an example: a situation where we have seen a man having a sexual fling, then discover that he is married, and that his wife knows his secret. In the worst kind of exposition, you might have this kind of interaction in the dialogue:

HE

I suppose there's no point in denying it. How did you find out?

SHE (cynically)

Mrs Bloggs on the corner saw you and phoned me. This is the fifth affair you have had in the past five years, and every time you try to make me believe I am imagining it. I remember that little blonde secretary you had. You used to race her off on the desk and you'd buy her presents on your visa card. You'd come home late every night saying how hard you were working, and I'd believe you. I was on my own every night. God, what a fool I was. And I always took you back and believed you. Four more times I did that, and every one of them was a blonde airhead. You told me every time that it would never happen again. Well I'm not putting up with it anymore.

This could go on forever. The point is, after fighting over five affairs, this couple would not be having this conversation with this amount of detail. They've had it too many times in the past. The wife is simply verbalising past history to convey information to the audience. Moreover, people rarely talk in monologues unless they're driven by strong emotional outbursts. This wife is cynical. It's just another affair in a marriage full of them. She knows he's unfaithful. She's more annoyed at herself for putting up with it. How much better if the interaction had played something like this:

HE

I suppose there's no point in denying it?

SHE

Please, have a little self-respect. God knows I'm trying to hang onto mine.

HE

Who told you?

SHE (cynical)

Does it matter? Maybe I've developed a sixth sense through experience. This is number six? Or is it five?

HE (weary)

Please . . .

SHE

What are you trying to do? Corner the market in blonde bimbos?

HE

I promise you, they don't mean anything.

SHE

They do to me. I've had five years of practice. And don't tell me it won't happen again. Let me tell you . . . it won't happen again. That's my promise.

There's nothing important in the first exchange that we haven't covered in the second. But the second exchange is more in keeping with a long-standing problematical relationship which is finally coming unstuck. What's more, the second exchange creates an undercurrent. There's a real sense that she's calling a halt to all this. An implied threat in a relationship always creates more tension than an explicit one.

If you have no choice but to state the obvious for the audience's benefit, at least remember that the characters don't know the audience is there. Don't put words in their mouths, force conversations on them that they would not be having in reality.

Constructing the scene

I won't dwell on the purpose of the scene, for I have already discussed it. Take on board, though, the fact that every scene in itself is a miniature story. It has a beginning, a middle and an end. Very often the audience might not pick up the scene until the middle; the beginning will have happened off-screen. But it's still there. However, very often the difficulties for an inexperienced writer are:

Where to locate the scene
How to begin and end it
What to put in it

What are the priorities? You need first to recognise the point of the scene. Does it advance the plot? Does it advance the relationship between the characters? Does it tell the audience something important? Is this a single piece of information? If it is, can you couple it with other developments to increase the dynamic range of the scene? Once you recognise these factors, you construct your scene for maximum dramatic impact. Your dialogue, location, entry and exit points from the scene will all be geared to that.

Having said that, I should warn you about a potential trap. Very often a new writer will start the scene too late, eliminating the chance to build both tension and intrigue before the denouement, or point of dramatic impact. Conversely, a scene may start too early. There may be quite a lot of trivial banter before a sudden change of mood leads to the denouement. Remember, if a piece of information is going to be conveyed from one character to another, that character carries into the scene, right from the start, an appropriate mood and attitude. You cannot start a scene with light banter and then have the character suddenly remember this earth-shattering news. So you need to construct your scene to feature the undercurrent, since this is all part of the progression towards that point of maximum impact. Once you reach that point, which might not be the actual information conveyed by one character, but rather the second character's reaction to it, there is no point in prolonging the scene—you will only lose the momentum.

In our 'Sally and Son' story, Sally is told by the doctor that she has a condition which requires surgery. You probably wouldn't bother showing her entering the surgery, saying hello, observing the doctor get his notes out, and so on and so forth. You'd set up a scene (or several) before this to show her anxiety, and her entering the doctor's rooms. You might pick up this scene by showing the doctor's awkwardness as he tries to tell her the bad news, then follow through on Sally's initial incredulity followed by her shock and despair. That's if you plan for Sally's plight to be the point of dramatic impact of the scene. If, however, what you are emphasising is the question, 'What is going to happen to her handicapped son?' then you might well pick up the scene with Sally's reaction, let the audience learn the news through the doctor's sympathetic interaction, and build to a point where we, the audience, realise with shock that Sally is alone, except for a handicapped child—and who's going to look after him? That jolting realisation would be the dramatic impact.

Locations must always provide more than simply a visual backdrop for a scene. You don't wait until you drive all the way to a clifftop with a stunning panoramic view to tell someone something which you would logically tell them while you're cleaning your teeth. Nor, unless there's a legitimate reason, do you stretch time and hold off telling someone something until you're in a more attractive place. As a writer you must look at the logic as well as the logistics involved. Perhaps you have a man who has important news to tell his wife. Obviously, if it's important, he will tell her the instant he gets home. But you have constructed your story in such a way that other action is taking place at the time he would normally be telling her. Your script has flown into an action sequence which takes up half that night. So you conveniently have the husband tell the wife this news before he goes to work the next morning. The audience knows that real people don't behave that way, and you've just lost them. However, if you preface his news with him saying that she was asleep when he got home; that he tried to wake her but couldn't; that he couldn't sleep himself, etc, etc, the audience will buy it. Even then, though, he would tell her the moment she woke up, not wait until he was ready to go to work.

The logical place is most often where a scene would be set. The exception to this is when you deliberately want the location to play against the interaction, as a way of creating a different dynamic in the scene. This location may be the choice of your character. A man may break off a relationship with a woman in a crowded place, a restaurant perhaps, knowing that she will not want to make a scene. This allows the writer to move away from the stereotyped 'How could you do this to me?' argument to something far more tense, but more low key.

Earlier in this chapter I said that the approach to dialogue

should be to eliminate as much of it as possible and tell the story visually. Let's go back to the doctor's office for a moment. Can we convey everything we've talked about with one piece of dialogue? We've said that there is already a set-up. We know about David. We've met Sally. We know she's going to the doctor. What about this:

SALLY stands looking out of the window of the surgery, but seeing nothing. Shock and disbelief on her face, she fights back the tears welling in her eyes. DOCTOR MORRIS looks uncomfortable, but full of compassion.

DR MORRIS

I'm so terribly sorry. It isn't usual at your age . . . I . . . is there anyone who . . .?

SALLY turns to him, sniffs back the tears and smiles stoically before shaking her head, resignedly.

Later on we'll find out the precise details, as Sally tells the DSS, or Annie. Already we, as the audience, know something is terribly wrong with this girl. Even the doctor feels bad. We know already she has a handicapped child. We ask ourselves what's going to happen to him? Is she going to die? We know all this, not from what we have heard, but from what we have seen. That's what film is all about.

Exercises

Step A: Write a scene simply in dialogue form. Decide before you start what your point of maximum dramatic impact is. Do not include any attitudes, any actions, any props or any setting. Simply create interaction through words. The scene should be fully developed with an appropriate lead-up to your point, and an appropriate natural finish to the scene.

Step B: When you have completed this, rewrite the scene including attitudes and action—the behaviour of the characters. Although you know what they're thinking and feeling, and what their body language is saying, I don't want you to include location, props or anything else. The purpose of Step B is to see how much dialogue you can eliminate, once you add attitudes and body language. Remember, your point of dramatic impact stays the same. Aim to cut your dialogue by at least 50 per cent.

Step C: Now do the scene for the third time. This time give it a location, props, visual aids, whatever you want, plus those elements you added at step B. The purpose of this step is to try to eradicate all dialogue. Most likely this won't be possible. To reach the point of dramatic impact will probably require someone saying something. However, if you manage to get your dialogue down to two exchanges, one from each character, and let the visuals tell the bulk of the story, you are now writing in pictures. You have also created subtext and you're more than ready for the next chapter.

9

Subtext and visual subtext

IS WHAT YOU SEE WHAT YOU GET?

Subtext and visual subtext are probably the most confusing areas for new writers. Some don't even know what they are—few know how to get them—yet they are what take your script and characters from the one-dimensional to the three-dimensional, whilst all the time remaining two-dimensional on the screen. What is the difference between the two? Subtext means quite literally what is beneath the text, below the surface, if you like. Most often it is contained within character and lies beneath dialogue. Visual subtext plays alongside the text but its specific purpose is to replace exposition, back story, plot elements, or any other device which might sit awkwardly in the script when expressed through dialogue. Let's examine them separately.

Subtext

It's too simple to say, as most of the people I meet in workshops do, that subtext is used 'When the character isn't telling you everything'. Sometimes the character isn't telling you anything—or doesn't think he or she is. Subtext operates on a number of levels, but basically it can be categorised as conscious, subconscious, and unconscious.

Conscious subtext

I use this simple game as a demonstration. I'm not telling you the truth—you know I'm not telling you the truth—I know that you know that I'm not telling you the truth—and you know that I know! Each of those statements represents a layer of conscious subtext in its most simplistic form. In each case, our attitudes are shaped, and changed a little, by unspoken realisations that we share. I call it Sara Lee scripting—'Layer upon layer upon layer'. On this conscious level, the subtext is governed and controlled by the character. Something is being held back. The audience may not know what it is, but is intrigued; or the audience may know exactly what the character is hiding, and shares the secret. Very often the character will be partially telling the truth, or avoiding it. The point is that more is being conveyed than is actually being expressed. What is conveyed may be additional and supplementary to what is being said, or it may be directly opposed to what is being said. When we talk of subtext on a conscious level, we are examining the dynamics created in a scene when two characters do *not* say what they mean, or at least not all that they are thinking. Yet they are still conveying information to each other in ways other than words. The point of the scene may well be within the subtext, which is being controlled by at least one of the characters. Let's say, for example, that the scene hinges on the realisation of one or both characters that they are falling in love, and they're afraid of the emotional consequences. The dialogue, if we want to bury the reality in the subtext and alter the dynamics, may be about something as mundane as a bus ticket. Both parties know precisely what they want to be talking about, but there is an unspoken agreement not to bring the subject up. Even so, when you write, the love scene dominates the conversation about the bus ticket. Woody Allen excels at writing hysterically funny angst-ridden scenes which are, in the subtext, poetic and often beautiful explorations of human emotions.

We've discussed already, in the preceding chapters on character and dialogue, the fact that few people are completely up front. Most of the human beings we encounter in our lives have secrets. Most will only allow you to see what they want you to see. Some, however, will give you a clue. They behave in a way which is contrary to everything they tell you. It's as if they are saying, 'See me, don't just listen to me.'

Subconscious subtext

If we move deeper, down to this next layer, we find that people will often give away secrets involuntarily, betrayed by their

subconscious. Most often, subconscious subtext is not supplementary but totally contrary to what is in the text. There's a
very old song from early this century entitled 'Your lips tell me
no-no, but there's yes-yes in your eyes'. Subtext. On this subconscious level, the subtext will generally be portrayed to the
audience visually, through body language. The point is, though,
that at this level the character is unaware that the body is saying
something which contradicts the words.

Thus, if we have a seemingly aggressive character claiming
to be unafraid, and ready for a fight—yet that character is
backing away towards the door—we understand through this
action that the person is afraid, or is running away from the
fight, and that the words mean nothing. Conversely, if a character claims to want nothing from another except to make peace,
yet is advancing confrontationally, fists clenched, the audience
(and probably the other character) is going to be saying, 'Back
off. You're lying.'

Quite often the body language which is physical can be
replaced simply by an emotional attitude, the attitude or mood
playing directly against the content of the dialogue. Subconscious subtext is often easier to write than conscious subtext,
for in the latter there's a degree of game playing by one or more
of the characters, and that can be quite difficult for the writer
to control. The subconscious level requires the writer's attention
to the directions in the script. Whilst I've urged you not to leave
out attitudes if they are pertinent, I would suggest that you don't
include specific actions unless they are pertinent and form part
of the body language of the subtext. Too often I see directions
in a script which say, 'He brushes the hair back from his eyes',
or 'She gets up from the table and moves to the sink'. Why? Is
he nervous? Is he furious that he didn't get a haircut? Has she
got cramps in her legs? Is the washing-up overdue? If the
movement directly enforces the mood, or point, of the dialogue,
it's irrelevant. If she says, 'I don't want to talk about this
anymore. I've got washing up to do', then of course she's going
to make that move and you don't need to confirm it. If, on the
other hand, she's saying, 'Okay, fine, let's sit here and discuss
it, I don't mind how long it takes', *then* makes the move to the
sink, away from the table, away from the confrontation,
we know that the action is revealing her true feelings. She
doesn't want to be at that table—she'd rather do anything, even
wash-up.

Unconscious subtext

This is a very deep and complex level of the script, which none of the characters is aware of, and yet which directly affects their behaviour. Often it will deal with concepts of morality and philosophy. It can only be controlled by you as the writer and it requires an ability to look deep into the souls of your characters. Most often you will find it in conjunction with seriously psychotic characters, and storylines with subplots which play on a number of levels. It can be dangerous if handled irresponsibly, for it usually raises controversial issues. In *The Silence of the Lambs* (Orion 1991), for example, we recognise easily the conscious and subconscious subtext in the interaction between Hannibal Lector and Clarisse. Yet what are the elements that drew both her and the audience towards a repellent cannibal? What was the writer saying about the compelling quality of pure evil without malice, and how attractive that appears to be to so many of us?

Sometimes a writer does not recognise the unconscious subtext within a work, yet it is irrefutably there. Be very careful about what you are trying to say at this level, and how deeply you bury it beneath the text.

A film, or television, drama can be much enhanced by subtext, yet so often it is accidental on the part of the writer, or it's the product of the actor and director who look beyond the words. You can and should, as the writer, include it in your script. It's a craft skill, and it hinges on how well you know your characters and respect them; nevertheless you can develop it with practice, along with all your other skills.

Visual subtext

Can a picture literally paint a thousand words? In film terms, it can certainly eradicate many hundreds of the boring, expository kind. We use visual subtext specifically to replace dialogue in the following areas:

1 When certain knowledge and relationships are already in place between the characters, but there is information that needs to be conveyed to the audience.

2 When one character is gleaning information about another, which that character is not going to give voluntarily.

Do not confuse it with visual text. Visual text refers to those essential pictures which in their own right propel the story forward in plot terms. A wrong suitcase taken at the airport; a gun concealed under a pillow and discovered accidentally; a piece of jewellery which is a clue in a murder and robbery. These visuals are as important to the telling of the story as the characters themselves. Visual subtext, however, works on a more hidden, more subliminal level, much like subtext operating below the dialogue. Let's look at examples of the two areas mentioned above:

1 *The pre-existing relationship which the audience needs to understand*: in a script I edited a while back was a complex relationship between a young real estate agent, whose character was established, and an old woman, Cecilia, who was not yet established. The storyline resulted in a conflict of interest for the young man, for he was acting for a developer and trying to buy up, dirt-cheap, the property of a woman he had known since childhood, who had been a close friend of his grandmother. The two women had been Tivoli chorus girls back in the war years. He, Steven, saw Cissy now as a surrogate grandmother. Cissy had heart problems, blood pressure problems, and so on. Still, she was a feisty old bird who refused to go to a nursing home.

You can see already how difficult and convoluted a scene this would be in dialogue terms. The scene carried two major story points; one plot—the attempt to take over an old woman's house for less than it was worth; and one character development—the conflict within Steven when he has to face his conscience over a deal which will disadvantage someone he loves.

The writer, a talented newcomer, had explained everything in dialogue, switching backwards and forwards from exposition to plot. The scene was extremely long and wordy. The first thing we did was to split the content of the scene over two locations, kitchen and lounge room.

In the kitchen we saw Steven putting on the kettle while Cissy warmed the teapot, the two of them working in tandem in a way which showed us, the audience, even though we'd never seen them together before, that these two had a warm long-standing relationship. We also saw Cissy's collection of medication on the top of the fridge, and Steven's frown as he realised that the tablets were untouched. Now we knew that he was full of concern for her. We saw the dilapidated state of the house, and a brochure on a beautiful new retirement home, both indicative of his trying to justify buying her out.

Passing references were made to each as he did a hard sell on her moving. She put out freshly made prune cookies, with an aside that they've been his favourites since childhood. We saw from the grimace behind his smile as he bit one that they aren't his favourites and never have been, but he didn't want to hurt her. In the lounge, while they drank their tea and talked about real estate, were established some old showbiz photographs, including one specific photo: two women, in their forties but still glamorous showbiz types. One of them was clearly Cissy. A young boy holds hands with both of them. From Steven's expression of recognition we knew it was him. Now Cissy noticed him looking at the picture and made a comment that his Nana had the best pins in the business and made a great principal boy, but that she (Cissy) always had the best boobs.

In screen time the two scenes took about a minute and a half, and appeared to be about Steven trying to persuade Cissy to sell her house, which she was balking at. But we learned just about everything we needed to know about their relationship and their past simply by seeing a few carefully placed props.

2 *The search for information which the character will not give voluntarily*: Almost every film contains one scene of this nature, where a character learns about another character through things left lying idly around; books which may show literary taste where none was suspected; or a whole range of more sinister things which disclose that the mild-mannered neighbour is, in fact, a lunatic serial killer. In the last example, don't confuse visual text with subtext. If the character recognises that this person is a serial killer, then those visual clues are text. If the significance goes unnoticed by the character, but the audience is racing ahead in putting two and two together, then it's visual subtext.

So often a carefully placed photograph (especially one that's been torn up and taped together again), an old soft toy, some souvenirs, books, records and paintings can tell us more about a character, or a past relationship, than the characters themselves would ever be prepared to verbalise. Yet writers persist in putting words into people's mouths and telling the audience rather than showing them. Never forget that your success as a screenwriter is dependant upon your ability to visualise; to tell a story in pictures. If you've come this far in the book, you must have recognised that talent within yourself. Don't be afraid to use it.

Exercises

a) *Subtext*: Take any scene that you have been working on. If you haven't yet started your script, then use a video of any film you enjoy. Now, without altering a word of the text, change completely the attitudes and body language of the characters. Make a note of how the meaning of the scene changes while the words remain the same. Do it a second time, with different attitudes and body language. Note how the scene changes again. Depending on the complexity of the relationship, there is a wide variety of possibilities. Whilst the information conveyed remains exactly the same, the motive, the emotional focus, and the interaction change dramatically so that each variation of the scene will be different and the audience will draw different conclusions. Can you see how important it is for you to know what you're trying to convey and build it into the subtext? A director and actors may alter the 'feel' and the truth of your scene without ever changing what you have written. There is *always* (if you have talent as a writer) more going on in your scene than what is simply being exchanged through dialogue.

b) *Visual subtext*: Henry is a divorced man with three children. He's bitter about his ex-wife, but loves his kids. Hopelessly inept at keeping house, he loves to cook, although he creates World War III in his wake. Nervous, shy, a solitary man who likes to fish, he invites Jane to his flat for dinner. She knows nothing about him, except that he seems nice. Write a scene in which she, and the audience, learn *all of the above* without Henry giving her any of the information we have mentioned. You may include subtext along with the visual subtext.

Now do the scene again without any dialogue whatsoever and convey the same information. (Yes, it is possible.)

10

The range of formats

A ROSE BY ANY OTHER NAME

When is a script not a script? When it is in any of the formats that will eventually lead to a script. There are various stages in the writing process. The more experienced you become, the more stages you are able to eliminate. Even so, you need to know exactly what each is and what function it has. We all understand what a first-draft script is, in theory at least, although most new writers have great difficulty in physically creating one. But what about the other formats we will be confronted with from time to time? What's the difference between a pitch and a synopsis? Exactly what is a treatment?

Let's look at all the various formats you may be asked to present in either film or television, define clearly what each is and determine when you might use it. I'll list them in order of length and the chronological place they might occupy in preparation. Incidentally, take note that all the formats for drama are written in the present tense, as if the story is unfolding in front of us, which of course it will be in visual terms.

The synopsis

This is a straightforward, chronologically ordered and encapsulated telling of your story in one or two pages. When you're already working with a production company or a producer, you might use a synopsis just to follow the story from A–Z. If,

however, you wanted a short document to send to a producer
with the hope of gleaning interest in your project, you would
send the following.

The pitch or teaser (usually what is identified as the synopsis)

You write this in a different style to the synopsis, and you do
not necessarily start with the plot. Most likely you would pitch
your main character first (remember the line, 'It's about this
person who . . .'). The aim of the pitch is to hook the reader
into wanting to read more, so generally you would not disclose
your ending, but rather leave a question mark over it, a sense
of intrigue. So, in a shorter form than you would actually use
(for brevity's sake), the pitch on 'Sally and Son' might look like
this:

Sally and Son

Sally Parr is a young battler with small dreams . . . a home, a
job, a husband. In reality she has a DSS single mum's pension
and David, seven years old, warm, loving, and seriously handicapped. When Sally is told that she needs major surgery, she
looks for someone to help her with David. But friends are scarce,
and family nonexistent. The DSS learns of her plight and tries
to take David away from her. They want to institutionalise
him—temporarily, they say—but Sally isn't about to take that
chance. She takes David and runs, moving from city to city. Not
caring about her own health, she stays one step ahead of the
DSS, afraid of losing her child. When Annie, another single
mother whom Sally pairs up with, is charged with negligence
following the death of her daughter, she turns back to drugs.
Sally must watch her only friend self-destruct. Annie's second
child is taken away by the State, and she suicides. Terrified that
something like this will be her fate in a few years' time, Sally
realises that she can either keep running forever or go back and
fight for her rights. But can one sick young woman without
money or education, driven only by her love for her child, take
on the system and win?

You can see that the pitch creates its own tension and
conflict and this is done in order to leave the reader wanting
more. It also starts with a sharp and succinct picture of the
person whose story it is; not a picture of what she looks like,

but what she wants, what she feels. It's probably the most useful single page you can ever write while trying to establish yourself as a writer, and you should practise pitch-writing at every opportunity.

The pitch or concept document

This is an enlargement on the pitch in that it first tells the reader *what* to expect . . . then goes on to outline *how* you will meet this expectation. It is used mostly for interesting networks or production companies in developing a series. Let's take *Neighbours*, for example. Your first page might start with a standard pitch of the idea, something like:

In every suburb of every town there's a Ramsay Street. And in that street, where you or I might live, there are <u>Neighbours</u>. Each household has its secrets, its loves, its conflicts. What happens when the <u>Neighbours'</u> lives spill into your own, and their problems become yours?

And so on. The next page, having pitched the idea in outline, would then pitch the timeslot, the demographic, the dynamics of the series, the expected world market. The page after that would probably sell the major characters, the one after would project short sketches for storylines. What this pitch does is encapsulate an entire outline for a potential series in a way which enables the reader to judge, from a very few pages, whether this idea is worth pursuing.

Storyline

This is a straightforward, no frills, expansion of your synopsis which gives a clear indication of who's in the story and what it is. It is most often used in television as part of the process of creating series or serial episodes.

The treatment

This one is a real problem to explain, and it's taken me a long while to come up with a succinct definition. It also has a slightly different meaning in film and television terms, so I will cover both:

Film

A treatment is the chronological (in screen time) unfolding of the story, generally without dialogue, paying particular regard to style, dynamics, mood, genre, colour, character and action. *It is what's happening on the screen in words.*

I've described it as 'generally without dialogue', though in fact sometimes you may be required to develop several scenes in dialogue form. If you remember that it is the screen visuals in words, and that what you write must be able to be shown, it will make life simpler. Most treatments contain such aberrations as, 'They met first in Berlin in 1963, when she was on a hiking trip, and they have not seen each other since'. This kind of material doesn't belong in a treatment (or in any other format for that matter). You can't show it, nor can a character say, 'We met first in Berlin in 1963 . . .', etc. However, you could say: 'Tentatively they explore their past relationship, reminiscing about their time in Berlin in 1963, over several cups of coffee.' That suggests a scene, a mood, something we can actually see happen on a screen.

When do you use the treatment? As a new writer, you probably don't. Any application for funding would need to be accompanied by a first-draft script (see Chapter 15). However, once you are a credited writer and you are ready to begin a new project with everything clear inside your mind, you would probably write a treatment and use it as your application for funding, asking for money to complete the first draft. It's quicker to write a treatment than a full script, since it is usually around 12–30 pages per screen hour in length. So, if you write a brilliant, succinct, colourful and visual treatment of around 35 pages, you may be given $10 000 or so on which to live while you write the script, which will probably keep you full time for five months or so. Despite their usefulness, most writers hate treatments because they are forced to lock down ideas and story and plot progressions that they would prefer to keep open at that creative stage. There's nothing to stop you digressing from the treatment when you write the first draft, as long as it's substantially the same story for which you are being funded. Still, most of us find it quite difficult to write present tense prose which will capture the vision we intend to present on the screen.

Television

The treatment for television is rarely used for a telemovie or teleplay. Most often it's a form used for a mini-series or a series.

Again, it breaks down the story and tells it as it would be seen on the screen. Only this time it does it in a scene-by-scene unfolding. It does not use scene headings, but each paragraph on the page indicates a separate scene and gives a clear idea of who is in it and where it is set. Whilst it doesn't need to have the same style as the film treatment, it must suggest the dynamic range of the story and clearly indicate what timeslot you are talking about.

Even a funding body would most likely allow your application to contain one hour of first-draft script, and the remainder in treatment form.

Once you have credits you will be able to do an entire treatment. The same applies for a series except that, if the idea is your original work, you would also include the elements I discussed earlier in this chapter in the pitch document, only more developed. You would do a full storyline on your opening episode, then full breakdowns of, say, half a page each, on your main characters and you would need to include at least seven, but preferably twelve, additional story outlines (synopses) so that the reader could see whether you have sufficient material for a series. Once you are a credited writer you will move further away from this form and more towards the pitch document form as a way of gleaning interest in developing your project.

The scene breakdown

This is precisely how it sounds. It breaks the story down chronologically into the scenes that will be seen on the screen, whether that screen be big or small, and is written in prose. Each scene has a heading and a number, just as it will have in your script. It is always used in television drama, and is either prepared by the writer or by the storyline team. It's essential for budget, cast and scheduling requirements. It gives everyone a blow-by-blow description, without dialogue, of precisely what your first-draft script will include. It won't have the nuances or subtlety that your script will have (one hopes) , but its application is practical. From a scene breakdown the reader can see instantly whether the structure works, what the dynamics are, whether the momentum is maintained. Because television is such a voracious animal, and because there simply isn't the time that there is in film production, the scene breakdown cuts down to a minimum the risk of a script not working.

In film it's generally a matter of personal choice, but I would

advise any new writer, especially one who has not tackled a full
length screenplay before, to do a scene breakdown. It will stop
you getting carried away with your characters and dialogue. It
enables you to say to yourself, 'Wait a minute, I've got them
here doing this, and they were just there doing the opposite'. It's
a very valuable tool. Its disadvantages are that doing it is
time-consuming and (in film) no-one is going to see it except
you. Most film writers don't do scene breakdowns, although if
they've written for television they certainly know how to, because
they get in the way of the stream of creative consciousness. We
jump straight in, once our idea is formulated, and start on a
first draft. Spending a week on a scene breakdown is nobody's
idea of fun. If we are honest though, we would concede that,
with experience, the scene breakdown becomes a mental process
that we have already completed in our heads. Thus we know
instinctively what scene comes after the one we're writing, who's
in it, and where it's located.

Thumbnail scene breakdown

This is useful at any stage of your development and sometimes
a script editor on your feature script will suggest you do one.
Briefly, it is a scene breakdown which supplies just one or two
lines about each scene, indicating the key elements. A full script
can be broken down, scene by scene, into two or three pages,
instead of 50 or more. You can read the one or two lines and
decide straight away whether it's a valid scene or a TC (tentative
cut), whether its point was what you intended, or whether it's
in the wrong place. Often you can identify a problem in this
short form that you can't see in the fully expanded script.

First draft

This is your script, in full, whether it be film or television. It is
told scene by scene, as it will appear on the screen, in a
combination of action and dialogue. Because there is so much
confusion about what to put in, what doesn't belong, how to
format it, what terms you should use, and so on, the following
chapter will take you through everything you need, except the
talent and the story, to create a first draft.

11

Formatting the first draft

IF IT LOOKS LIKE A SCRIPT . . .

If it looks like a script, reads like a script . . . there's a good chance it's a script! When you come to a script as a producer, an editor, or even as an assessor for a funding body, your first impressions cannot help but be coloured by the way a script *looks*, before you've had a chance to respond to its content.

The minute I see a film script which starts ACT ONE—FADE IN I know I'm looking at the work of an amateur writer, self-taught from American how-to books. That, by the way, is part of an American television format. Australian film scripts don't fade in, fade out. Australian television scripts deal in segments, not acts.

So, what should your script look like? What terms should you use? What is included and what isn't?

Let's start with a glossary of terms that are essential for you to be familiar with in putting your script on paper, and see how you apply them in practice. Notice that most of these terms are capitalised. Later in the chapter we'll discuss other ways to make your script look more professional.

Glossary

ACTION   This does not just mean car chases or fights. It means the part of your scene which is not dialogue. If your scene starts with the words, 'FRED and DULCIE sit at the table staring at the tablecloth', they may appear to be doing nothing, but in fact this is still called action. It is also called 'the big print'. It must not contain anything which cannot be shown on the screen, no references to their past, to incidents which have affected them, etc. It should contain a clue to their attitudes since these can be shown on the screen and set the mood for the scene. So you might add to your action, 'FRED with suppressed anger, DULCIE with weary contempt', which then can be clearly shown by actors and director to the audience. This way we know what mood each is in before a word of dialogue has been exchanged.

In a film script, paradoxically, the action or big print is always written in ordinary old capital and lower case type. The exceptions are character names and essential props, e.g., a large GREY EAGLE flies through the window. You'll see in some American scripts that adjectives appear in capitals in 'the big print', e.g., she screams LOUDLY. We are not in America.

In television the big print is often just that—all capitals. However it's wise before writing to check to see what method is used by the production company you are dealing with, since there is an increasing tendency towards adopting the film format. Why are the characters' names always in capitals? So that the production manager and any other reader knows precisely who is in every scene, even when they are not speaking. For example, even with extras you would write . . . a SMALL CROWD gathers, so that the reader knows at a glance that they are also required in the scene.

CU   This is the abbreviation for close-up. ECU is extreme close-up; MCU is medium close-up. *Use these sparingly.* You'll find in American screenwriting guides that the writers tend to call every shot for the director. Remember, the case studies for these books are Academy Award-winning screenplays written by the top screenwriters. They can afford such indulgences as directing the director; we cannot. It isn't the writer's job to tell the director how to shoot the script. You should *never* suggest camera shots unless it is imperative for the scene and the story that there be, say, an ECU at a specific time.

CUT TO   This means, literally, stop shooting one thing and shoot another. The director knows when to do that without your help, so don't spell it out, especially at the end of a scene when there's nothing to do but cut, unless you want a feud with the director before you've even met. However,

JUMP CUT TO   is a useful direction and you probably would employ that term. A JUMP CUT occurs when the 'out' or tail of one scene throws directly to the top, or head, of another scene, usually with the same character(s), but involving a jump across a period of time and probably also location.

DISSOLVE You might use this term if you felt it was essential. It's a soft transition from one scene or image to another, a blending which takes the hard edge off the cut. What you would most likely use is the TIME LAPSE DISSOLVE. This most often happens when you have a scene that you want to break in the middle and then pass over a lot of time. It isn't regarded as two scenes, though one is a little later than the other, if the characters and location are identical in both.

Let's look at an example in a hypothetical scene.

43 INT KELLY'S LOUNGE NIGHT 43

KELLY puts the tray of coffee down on the table and starts to pour. MARK never takes his eyes off her. The sexual tension between them is overwhelming. She steadies her hand to put two sugars in the cup, then finds her voice.

                    KELLY

Anything else?

TIME LAPSE DISSOLVE.
Kelly's panties drape the coffee pot, her bra is in Mark's coffee . . . clothes are strewn everywhere. KELLY and MARK lie intertwined on the floor, glowing in the aftermath of great sex.

              MARK (teasingly)

How about some after-dinner mints?

You can see that by dissolving through the foreplay and the sexual act we have tightened the scene and played it for romantic comedy. I personally like time lapse dissolves and find them useful for moving through extraneous, but natural, interaction. When shooting, this scene would probably be designated 43 and 43(a), because there would have to be a break to allow for the disrobing, etc.

However, most script software packages don't allow for that kind of deviation from the norm. You could number the scenes 43 and 44, put the TIME LAPSE DISSOLVE at the end of 43 and pick up 44 with your first words in the big print being: 'An hour later . . .' You would certainly make it two scenes if MARK had, say, gone home, or the coffee things had been cleared and KELLY had changed clothes—in other words if the scene was not a direct continuation of the one we had dissolved through.

EXT and INT   These are the abbreviations for *exterior* and *interior*. After recording your scene number, you will use one of these terms. Your scene heading will be typed entirely in capital letters. For example:

1 EXT DIRT ROAD—OUTBACK (NQ 1965)   DAY   1

The underlining is not essential, it's just a personal preference of mine. Everything else is essential. The material in brackets gives the producer and director a sense of time and place at the head of the script. You only need to say it once.

2 INT LIVING ROOM (FRED'S HOUSE)   DAY   2

It is not just the interior of Fred's house which heads the scene, but a specific location within his house: the actual place where the cameras will be set up.

I looked at a script recently which had only two scene headings throughout the entire script: INT MT ISA and EXT MT ISA. Obviously we can see that the first is wrong—unless we are Peer Gynt and have somehow stumbled into the 'hall of the mountain king', having first fallen down a mine shaft. The second is equally wrong. It should read EXT STREET or EXT THE BANK or whatever the specific location is. The writer should have established MT ISA once only, in brackets. It is then taken as read that we are still there unless the writer moves the characters to another town. For the record, a scene is also either designated DAY or NIGHT in your scene heading. If it's dawn, specify that in your action/big print, likewise dusk. For production purposes there are no halfways.

FX   This means effect. SFX means sound effect. For example: 'SFX—a phone rings in another room'.

INTERCUT   You will probably use this only in a television script, again because preferred script software packages (if not your own, then certainly the producer's) will not be able to read it. The intercut is the cutting between two directly linked scenes; where you cut backwards and forwards between one and the other. The classic example is of two people having a conversation on the phone. If you are in a television studio, shooting on video, you would head it thus:

21 INTERCUT JANE'S BEDROOM/DAVE'S KITCHEN NIGHT 21

Then you would just write the scene with the dialogue; every time Dave spoke the director would shoot him in his kitchen, and when Jane spoke, shoot her in her bedroom. This can be done because video television employs four cameras, so it's possible to shoot both conversations at the one time. However, in Australian film production, it's rare that the budget will allow even so much as two cameras, two cameramen, two focus pullers and so on. Moreover, you can't cut from one camera to the other in film as you can in video. So the scenes would be shot on different sets or locations, and generally on different days. It's this type of confusion about what a separate scene is which most often leads to erroneous scene headings and makes the reader assume that some writers don't know their craft.

MONTAGE   A montage is a collection of visual images in different locations; small scenes without dialogue and usually musically underscored. Thus it is entirely made up of action/big print. It is used to denote the passing of time or place . . . perhaps a character moving from childhood to adulthood . . . or the development of a relationship, or an action sequence. If you see a sequence in a film where the characters, for example, are travelling first by car, then plane, then ship, that is a montage. We cover entire continents in about thirty seconds instead of having scenes which have no real point, or having our character walk out of the door in Australia, and in another door in France, which is a jump cut. It can save a lot of extraneous scenes, particularly in situations where you would be repeating information at each step. But it should be used sparingly. Some producers have absolute phobias about montages, not least because they are expensive to shoot and you have very little screen time to show for them. You can give your montage a scene number, but then you will need separate numbering on each of your visual images, because each will constitute a separate scene on the shooting schedule. Alternatively, you can number images, as in the example following, though some script software (e.g., *Scriptor*), will not accept this.

Basically this is what your montage will look like on the page. Let's use our Sally story again.

22-26 MONTAGE. (UNDERSCORED ONLY)   22-26

---

22   INT DSS OFFICE   DAY
     SALLY argues with the CLERK, getting angrier at every
     word. A SUPERVISOR enters and joins in the argument.
     Now SALLY fights harder, believing they're ganging up
     on her. Finally she storms out. The CLERK and
     SUPERVISOR are not impressed.

23   INT SALLY'S LOUNGE   NIGHT
     DAVID, confused, is throwing a tantrum. SALLY grabs
     him, calms him, holding him to her. We see her own
     growing desperation.

24   INT SOCIAL WORKER'S OFFICE   DAY
     SALLY pleads with the SOCIAL WORKER. But the
     compassionate smile and shake of the head show she is
     getting nowhere.

25   INT SALLY'S BEDROOM   NIGHT
     DAVID is asleep in the bed they share. He looks peaceful,
     angelic. SALLY watches wistfully from the doorway. She's
     clearly in physical pain.

26   INT BATHROOM   NIGHT
     SALLY reaches into the old cabinet and takes a few
     painkillers from a bottle. She swallows them with water
     from her cupped hand. She catches sight of her face in
     the cracked mirror, drawn, pitiful. The well bursts, she
     starts to cry.

What we've done with this montage is:

1   Pass over several days in Sally's quest to find help with David
2   Move the character from angry and confrontational to des-
    perate
3   Show Sally's physical deterioration at the same time as
    enforcing her relationship with David

You can see how useful this device can be, eliminating the
problems of repetition that might have been involved in scenes
22 and 24 where the same information was conveyed to different
people. However, I would expect this montage to follow at least
one fully developed confrontational scene with the bureaucracy
in which we see Sally in full flight.

POV   You'll use this term quite often. It means point of view
and it is used in a script to denote the view, the outlook as seen
literally through the character's eyes. It's one time when shot

calling for the director is permissible. So, if a character goes to the window to look out, and you want the audience to see what the character sees, you would say 'Character A's POV'. Don't confuse it with attitude. Your entire script may be written from A's point of view, but that's attitudinal, and a different thing entirely.

OOV   This stands for out of view and there is often confusion in the writer's mind as to whether to use OOV or VO, the latter standing for voice-over. But it is actually quite simple. If your character is physically required, but not seen, then their dialogue is OOV. An example would be: Your scene is set in a bedroom. One character is in bed, the other is supposedly in the bathroom down the hall. You may not in actual fact have a bathroom set, but nevertheless the two characters are going to have a conversation. So, the character heading for the bathroom is OOV because this person is physically required for the shooting of the scene. If you have someone on the radio, or on the other end of a phone, or in someone's thoughts speaking, then they would probably be recorded separately, audio only, and you would use VO.

SUBJECTIVE CAMERA   There is a subtle difference between this and POV. It usually means that an entire scene is shot with the camera performing in place of the character. You might use this device, as one writer I've been working with has, in a scene where, say, a girl is being viciously attacked. We don't see any part of the person attacking her. Instead we see the attack, through the camera lens, as if through the attacker's eyes. In other words, the camera becomes the attacker, moving in and out threateningly, and the girl reacts to it as she would to a real person. It's a device used often in thrillers and horror films, and it can sometimes add great dramatic impact to more serious genres.

These are the major terms you will need in constructing your script, and you should familiarise yourself with them before you start to write.

Writing the action

Now that you know how to format your script, what belongs and what doesn't? Most often the major mistakes occur in the action, the big print. So let us look at two scene headers (i.e. action) which tell us the same thing: one incorrect, one correct.

10 INT DOCTOR'S   **DAY   10**

This is the doctor's waiting room. The doctor's name is Doctor
Morris. He has a nurse, Nurse Philips, but we don't see her.
There are six PEOPLE waiting to see the doctor. They are
PATIENTS. One of the patients is a young woman.

She is fair-haired but plain and she is twenty-two years old.
She has been coming to this doctor for years. Now she is in
pain and nervously waiting for her test results. She is a single
mother. Her little boy, David, who is handicapped, is with her.
He is seven so she was only fifteeen when she had him. Her
name is SALLY PARR.

I have included as many aberrations as I can in that little
monstrosity, though I have actually seen headers to scenes which
are far worse. Forget the fact for a moment that we would
already have met and known Sally within the context of our
story. This is just an exercise.

The scene should have read more like this:

10 INT DOCTOR MORRIS'S SURGERY (WAITING ROOM) DAY 10

SALLY, 22, down but not out, waits nervously. In her hand she
clutches a pensioner's health card. At her feet her son DAVID,7,
struggles with a simple puzzle that most two-year-olds could
master. She smiles encouragingly through her pain. Other
PATIENTS watch the child judgementally, or try to ignore him
behind magazines.

Can you see the difference? Everything in the second example
can be shown on the screen. The audience will absorb the scene
visually plus all of that information without a word being
uttered. Sally's on a pension. She's in pain. Her child is handicapped. There's a strong bond between them. Other people are
judgemental. She ignores them. Her attitude is that of someone
who won't be beaten—down, but not out. The action in the
second example tells us all that. The first scene tells us nothing.
The second is also loaded with visual subtext. I will say it again
for the second and final time. Nothing goes in the big print that
can't be shown on the screen.

Layout

Your script should have margins of at least 2.5 centimetres on either side, and the same top and bottom. Your scene headings run the full tab width of your page, as does the action. Some script packages work only off single spacing. Double spacing is too spacey for a script and is misleading as to length. One-and-a-half spaces looks good on the page. More important is to ensure you have a double space between the end of action and character name when you move to dialogue, and at the end of dialogue before you recommence action.

Character names (always capitalised) are best centred, or at least indented to the halfway mark on the line. (I actually think this looks better, because dialogue is also indented, and character names then tend to be more centre of dialogue, rather than the page.) For dialogue I use the preset double tab that is in my word processing package, but it must be indented by 12–15 spaces, and should not run the full width to the end of the line. (See Chapter 8 for example.) If you're a new writer, don't go rushing off to buy one of the many software packages designed for scriptwriting. They are a luxury item. It's true that you are able to give one single command which will then allow the package to tab, move to upper case, centre, underline, tabulate, and do everything but bring you a cup of coffee or write your script. In reality, any reasonable word processing software package, or even a decent typewriter, will suffice. I personally don't have a script software package, although I keep meaning to get one. Unless you have money to spare, promise yourself that it's something you will get when you sell your first script . . . if other priorities don't come up first.

In certain television shows, which are entirely studio shot and therefore on video (this could include sitcoms, serials, children's drama), the format for dialogue is different. Your character name would go on the left hand side of the page, always in capitals. Your dialogue would then be indented and all subsequent lines of dialogue indented as well. For example:

SALLY   I doubt that I would ever actually be in a sitcom, but
         it's possible, and you might have to write me like this.
         But **always** check with the production company.

Protecting the script

The greatest fear of any writer is losing control of the script. Yet it is inevitable if you write professionally, for the writing process is simply the giving birth. Now your baby has to go out into the big wide world where it may well be kidnapped and have to grow up very fast. You can't hang on to your script. Accept that as fact. Letting go is a natural part of the writing process, just as it is of life. You can, however, give your script a certain amount of protection without encroaching on the areas of those who will take over the various aspects of production.

Be specific. This is important. Don't assume that anyone will know what you are talking about. Cover yourself if it's an important area in the script. Whilst you should never fill your action with descriptions of how a room looks (it's an art director's job to interpret that), when a piece of furniture or a prop can make or break a scene, make sure you signal your intent.

Let me give you two examples. I had to write a story in which a nun was put into prison. The nun was to have as a prop (subsequently destroyed by another prisoner) a bible which meant the world to her. She actually had dialogue describing how old and special this bible was. When I saw a rough edit of the episode, the nun was carrying a paperback version of the *Good News Bible*—which is the modernised, abbreviated, King James, Church of England version. I hit the roof. How could this happen? Quite simply, it hadn't occurred to me that anyone, not even the props department, would give a nun a paperback bible, especially when it was specified otherwise. But 'props' rarely read dialogue. They look through the big print. I should have specified 'a bible, very old, leather-bound, beautiful'. I should have protected my intent. Five extra words would have avoided a travesty.

When I played Mrs Meggs in the film *Ginger Meggs* (John Sexton Prods/Hoyts 1982), I had to return from a shopping outing with my basket full of groceries for the family. What was in that basket? Bottles of Coca Cola and packets of chips, that's what. Nothing else. Mrs Meggs is trying to feed a family on very little money, yet that's what she bought them to eat. The writer should have specified, 'Essential items only in the shopping basket show that money is tight'. Mind you, even if Mrs Meggs had had millions of pounds, she still wouldn't have bought coke and chips and nothing else.

Some people will say it doesn't matter, nobody notices those things, who cares? Believe me, if it's your script being bastardised, you will care. So don't assume *anything*.

Similarly, know when not to be too specific. Your descriptions of places, your action/big print, can often be a drawback. You are trying to convey an idea, a mood, a look, not say to a prospective producer that this script is going to cost a fortune to make. Don't specify '500 extras', say 'a crowd' or 'people' gather. Don't specify a Rolls Royce being written off in a car crash, say 'upmarket car'. Don't disadvantage your script by ever saying it *must* be one thing, when it could just as easily be something else.

If your script looks like costing ten million dollars to make, and you've been told that nothing over three million even gets read any more, then don't despair. Look at your story again. Most often a story can be kept intact at the same time as eliminating expensive trimmings.

Although you shouldn't call the camera shots for the director, you can suggest a style, a look, which will lead the director to the shot you wanted in the first place. Say you start your action with something like: 'Tortured, brooding, David's face seems to fill the entire screen', wouldn't you expect to get the same result as, 'Open on very tight ECU of David's tortured brooding face'? And this way, you won't get the director's back up for giving him orders.

Once you've written your first draft, doublecheck everything we have covered. Now put the script away somewhere where you will not be tempted to look at it. For the next four weeks forget all about it. This isn't an indulgence, it's a necessary separation process between writer and script. Four months might even be better, but who has that much patience? What you will do in that four weeks is (hopefully) move your viewpoint imperceptibly from the subjectivity of the writer to the objectivity of the reader.

PART 3

The completed script:
Now the fun really starts

12

Revising the first draft

OUCH! THE PAIN OF REWORKING THE SCRIPT

Four weeks later: you've reread the script and you can't believe
what's on the page. What happened to your brilliant, fast-moving
masterpiece? What gremlins were let loose to reduce it to an
over-expository, pretentious dirge? If we're honest, we are all
appalled when we see the traps we have fallen into, particularly
when we went to such pains to avoid them. If it's any consola-
tion, it happens to all writers who are objective about their work,
so you are not alone.

However, there is no need to feel despondent or depressed.
Just as you had to learn to work the script, now you have to
learn to rework it.

Reworking the script is an important part of the first-draft
process. It means eliminating extraneous dialogue, sharpening
up the big print, adding extra momentum and dynamics to your
last act. Sometimes it's a question of 'tweaking'—an extra adjective here, a scene location change there. The main element in
the reworking is that the writer must come fresh to the work,
which is why a minimum four-week break is essential. You'll be
astounded at how much of your script is a total surprise to you.
There will be great chunks of dialogue that you don't remember
writing. There will be scenes that seem to have come out of thin
air. It's natural, don't panic. Reworking is not the same as
rewriting. You will do that when you come to your second draft.
At second draft stage a good script tends to change shape quite
dramatically. One would expect, though, that unless you are

119

bitterly unhappy about your first draft, you wouldn't be contemplating a second draft until someone, somewhere, has given you objective and professional feedback. Often a second draft will have to meet the needs of an interested producer, and that will mean a whole new set of considerations. This first-draft reworking is still going to see you wind up with a first draft, but one that is bathed and powdered and all dressed up for the big trip to market.

This chapter will serve as a checklist to help you identify the problems and find the solutions, applying the techniques we've already talked about in a practical way. So let's look at all the problem areas, through some examples posed by our hypothetical writer in no particular order, and see how we rework them.

Character

Problem: The two main characters don't connect. Their relationship seems artificially imposed by me. Because of that, the way they end up together is unsatisfying, even to me.

Solution: Have you clearly identified their wants and needs? Do *they* have any inkling of what's driving them?

Remember, an incident, or a series of incidents that constitutes a plot or storyline, isn't sufficient to keep two people together once the storyline is resolved. If they don't fill a gap in each other's lives, then they don't really belong together. Examine the possibility of having them part. It's not a cheat for the audience if the audience also senses they don't really belong together. Conversely, go back to the psychological profiles you've constructed for them and try to identify the quality that attracted them to each other. If it's missing, incorporate it by adding that element to the character interaction or to the subtext. It may be an attitudinal problem, or simply a matter of clarifying motivation. Remember, if you change an attitude that's part of the character's makeup halfway through the script, then there must be a legitimate reason for the character growth.

Problem: My lead character seems to have lost the plot. The set-up works okay, but then in the second act he just seems to wander around with things happening to him over which he has no control.

Solution: You've set the character up to be passive rather than active. Remember that a passive character can be positive, just as an active character can be negative, but when we ask, 'Whose story is it?' then the character you identify must be controlling the action, even if it's in a negative way for example: running away from a situation. The problem is probably in the first-act turning point. Go back to that point and note how your character is propelled into the second act. If it's through something that happens against his will, or outside his control, then move him from passive to active by either having him fight against the situation at the same time as he's looking for a way out, or have him take control and use what's happening, consciously initiating responses in the action. You must not, however, simply have your character caught off guard and swept away by action that someone else, presumably the antagonist, is controlling, unless you plan a major revelation in the second-act turning point, and a total turnaround for the character in the third act. In that case you must still set your character up in the second act as an active character who has become a victim through circumstances outside his control, and he should still rail against his victim status.

Summary: There are literally dozens of problems that beset characters, and almost always it's because there is no clear identification of attitude or wants and needs.

Often you may have set the character up properly within the parameters of your story and then, in the writing, made changes to the plot. If you do that, you've got to accommodate your character's reaction. You can't simply impose your will over the character's. The most common example of this occurs in nine out of ten thrillers when a character, usually the female, goes to a place where she knows the killer is likely to be waiting for her, enters the dark room, climbs the stairs, or whatever. We know that in real life she would have run a mile, or called the police. We all recognise that she is acting totally out of character, but it's not through fear, or panic; it's simply because the writer wants it that way. The writer has no idea how to handle the story progression if she goes to the police. From that point on, unless you've set up a genuinely believable factor within her personality that convinces us she can't go to the police, you have lost your audience.

Structure

Problem: I can't get out of my second act and into my third. There's no turning point. Can't I just have an elongated second act with a short resolution at the end?

Solution: In a word, no. The turning point is there, it's just that
you haven't identified it. Perhaps you haven't even written it, but
it is implicit in a character's change of attitude or in a character
initiating a different action. Accept first of all that it's there, now
let's go looking for it. What is the moment when your characters
stop what they are doing in the second act, and start to do
something completely different? Examine it once you've found
it. If it has happened because they've changed their minds, their
attitudes, fallen in love or whatever, then there was a moment
of recognition before that, and that's your turning point. Pinpoint it, now build the scenes leading to it with extra momentum, keeping the central question in mind. Remember: turning
point is just that; there has to be a turnaround in character, or
action, or both. If it's so subtle that even you missed it, then
work on the catalyst. Do you recall, in the chapter on structure,
that we talked about a catalyst in the subplot forcing the turning
point in the main storyline? In that case Sally was on the run,
the subplot was the Annie story and it was Annie's suicide which
caused Sally to make the decision to go back. Her going back
moved us into act three, a change of direction, but if Annie
hadn't suicided (the catalyst) Sally might never have made the
decision. Look at your subplot: is there something you can use
which can be built into the catalyst? If not, write a plot sequence
which might serve the same purpose.

Problem: I wrongly identified my first-act turning point. Now I
discover, on rereading, that I've got an overlong first act, and
my turning point comes halfway through my script.

Solution: This is in fact a genuine problem . . . mine. For two
years I have identified the first-act turning point in a script of
mine as being an incident on page twelve, only to discover when
I started writing this book that the turning point is something
else entirely, and it comes on page 50. (Incidentally, I'm the only
one to have found it, although two producers and a director
recognised something as being not quite right.) I missed it
because my set-up was full of intrigue and conflict and moved
at a good pace with a number of plot points, one of which I
believed was the turning point. Now, I don't have any choice
but to completely rework the first act. A turning point can come
early. A few films break the rules and throw the turning point
at the audience before any real set-up. *Presumed Innocent*
(Warner Bros 1990) is one that comes to mind. But no script
can get away with a set-up that takes half the film. Once I rework
the first act, that will affect the second act which will now be

short of material, so some of the interaction will need to be moved across the turning point from act to act. But then I will need to take on board the fact that the attitudes and reactions are going to be different because the turning point has already taken place. It's major reworking.

Summary: Chances are that the structural problems you have will be either directly related to the turning points themselves, or to the loss of direction in the linear storytelling. If you already have your first draft in place and did not do the four page outline we talked about in Chapter 6, now is a good time to do it. It will help you cut through the gilding and strip your story back to basics. Losing sight of your actual story, or confusing it with your theme, or concept, can lead to very muddled structuring and it helps sometimes to write your story in just a few lines and tape it to the top of your PC monitor. In the following chapter I'll show you several editorial tricks for finding and identifying problem areas.

Dialogue and exposition

Problem: I've got several scenes in a row, full of long speeches. I can't cut them back because it's all information the audience has to know before I get into the action, but it's exposition after exposition.

Solution: Most often, what a writer thinks is essential for an audience isn't. Often the writer has created such a terrific back story that he/she can't bear not to include it. Thus we end up with:

A

What about your dad?

B

We don't talk to each other any more. It's been like that for ten years or more. When I was fourteen I made the A grade rugby team at school. That was the first time he ever really approved of me. His dream had been to be a professional rugby player but his father was a mean old bastard who kept him working on the farm when he should have been training. Anyway, he got a try-out for

a team and he broke his leg when he jumped from the
tractor, and never got his chance. So he wanted to fulfil
his dream through me. But I was more interested in the
music, so I started missing practice sessions. Eventually
I got dropped from the team and that was the end. I
don't think he really spoke to me after that.

You may think that's all essential information, but basically it's
just back story. All the audience needs to know is that B is
estranged from his father, and to have an inkling of why. So,
much more succinct is:

A

What about your dad?

B (guardedly)

We . . . er . . . we don't talk. It's, it's an expectations
thing. He wanted me to be something he couldn't be. I
guess neither of us could hack it.

Not only have we cut the exposition, but we've created subtext.
If the other scene is really providing essential information for
the audience, then bleed it in over a number of scenes, and let
a number of characters introduce it, so that the audience is party
to deducing the whole story. If you have to have a long speech,
it's justification should be that you're examining the emotional
makeup of the character, not the back story. You might want a
quiet moment when B pours his heart out to A, the first time
he's told anyone the full story. But then what he should be
expressing is the hurt, the anger, the confusion over his rejection
by his father, not the fact that his father broke his leg and missed
his try-out.

Problem: My dialogue reads really well, but somehow my characters are talking at each other, not interacting through the
dialogue.

Solution: This is probably going to sound like another of those
weird things I have said from time to time, nevertheless: are
your characters listening to each other? You may have found
their voices, they may know what they're saying, but are they
relating to what the other character is saying? Real interaction
through dialogue comes from one character reacting to what the

other is saying, and connecting through a direct response to the words. That means the characters really have to listen to each other. They can't have neatly pre-formed one liners created by you waiting to trip off the tongue the second the other character shuts up. My guess is that there is a lack of connection between speeches. Just as there must be a connection, a progression between scenes in order to build momentum, so the same is true of dialogue. If you want interaction between your characters through dialogue, then they must continue to respond directly to the previous speech and the thought or feeling behind it. So each response carries an exponentially expanding wealth of ideas and feelings. Of course, use the disconnection method if you want to create a sense of alienation, even isolation, amongst your characters. In this situation it is not so much what the characters say to each other, as the fact that the speeches will stand on their own, unresponsive to what has been said before, and will build a picture of two people who don't communicate even when they speak.

Summary: I can't stress enough how important it is to remember that the characters don't know they are in a film or a television show. You have to take their feelings and thought processes on board and respect them even if they are not your own. Many times I've edited out a really great line and had to explain to the writer that it's a fabulous line, but it doesn't belong in that character's mouth. Have conversations with your characters in your head. Know their minds inside out. Never put a single word in their mouths that wouldn't naturally be there. Always work your dialogue out loud, and always make sure your characters are listening to each other. They don't have to listen to you. You're the writer, and you don't exist as far as they are concerned.

Length

Problem: My feature film script is far too long. I need to cut at least a third (60 pages) from it. How can I do that without rewriting the whole script?

Solution: I don't think you can. My personal experience is that 'trimming'—tightening of all scenes and removal of extraneous dialogue and big print—can cut back perhaps 25 per cent, or around 35 pages. A script that's running at around three hours of playing time (180 pages) needs a total rethink. There are very few epics being made any more, even for the international market. The idea of a three-hour feature film for the Australian market just won't work. The first question I would be asking is, 'Do I genuinely have too much material here for a feature film? If so, can I add some secondary storylines, or develop the ones I have, and look at this as a four-hour mini-series?' In other words, you may have wrongly identified your medium in the first place. If that is not the case, and you want to continue with your script as a feature, you are going to have to restructure and write a second draft before you can field it out to the market. No producer is going to look at a script from a first-time writer running at 180 pages. Do your four page outline. Don't say it won't fit on four pages; make it. Now look at what you have left out. The chances are it is extraneous and can be cut. If a lot of it is exposition and character development, then build the subtext and let it carry the weight while you cut down on the text. Look at your set-up. Have you given the information to the audience once, and then repeated it in a different way? If you wanted to show that someone is accident-prone, for example, would you write four or five sequences where the character falls, knocks things over, whatever, because one sequence would not tell us this is a *recurring* element in the character? In actual fact, all you'd need is one sequence, then a scene in hospital casualty where everyone clearly knows this person, and the attitude is 'Not again!' Later you might have someone hiding all the breakables when the character visits. Subtext again, and the elimination of about 15–20 pages of set-up. Be brutally honest about what is necessary to tell your story. Start with that when you rewrite, and only add what your script will allow.

If you have plot sequences that are not essential to the telling of your primary storyline, cut them out. If they contain one or two lines of dialogue which are stepping stones in the plot development, give them to another character, one involved in the main storyline. Don't try to cut whole scenes, or sequences without reshaping the entire structure. You'll probably need to go to a thumbnail scene breakdown to look at what you need to keep. You may even discover an entirely different way to tell the story, changing the mood and possibly even the genre of the film. It's a big task, but it's important to realise that you are starting over. So approach the second draft as if it is a brand new script and then you'll discover the same magic in the story that convinced you to write it in the first place.

Problem: My film script is 75 pages long, and I've told the entire story. What can I do to pad it out to a marketable length?

Solution: Padding means precisely that, superfluous weight that the script would be better off without. I know that many scripts are padded with lots of extraneous dialogue and scenes that just fill up time, but to me that's just a sign of poor craftsmanship on the part of the writer. A good subplot, however, is not padding. It stands on its own merits and reinforces both the primary storyline and the theme. See if there is room for a subplot (some stories are so linear that there isn't) or, if you already have one, see that you have developed it to the fullest, giving it its own three-act structure, and its own dynamics. If not, do your four-page exercise on the subplot and see where it might be opened up to provide the additional material you need. Also, look closely at your script on the page. It might be 75 pages, but if it contains action sequences which you have not broken down, then these will add to the running time. For example, a scene which includes, 'Montage of car chases over the entire city with lots of smashes and narrow escapes', is two lines on the page, but could be up to ten minutes of screen time. The most famous line of understatement and underdevelopment in a script comes from *Gone With the Wind* when the entire civil war sequence was written in the script as 'and the battle raged'. Certainly the screen time was in no way related to the words on the page.

Summary: A good script runs for as long as it's meant to, as long as it takes to tell the story. However, the market requires a minimum and maximum time in order to assess budgets, programming aspects and so on. If your script is running between 90–125 pages, don't touch it. It's a first draft, and you will be rewriting anyway. Often producers are more nervous when a script is too short, since they can't see the potential for change. If it's too long, but manageable, they'll adopt the approach that you'll tighten it at the second draft. The main concern is to be certain in your own mind that you've told the story you wanted to tell as sharply and visually as you can.

Tweaking and polishing

You may be happy enough with your first draft to send it out for feedback, but have a close look at it before you do. Is it formatted properly? Are your scene numbers correct? Have you cleaned up all your typos? Did you do a spellcheck (preferably not with a word processing package that gives you American spelling)?

A polish is a smoothing of the rough edges. You may see that your 'big print' action is convoluted, or over-explanatory, or contains descriptions that can't be shown on the screen. Now's the time to clean it up. You might find dialogue that sits awkwardly. Sometimes only two or three word changes are necessary to make it flow. Tweaking is even less involved. It usually means exchanging one word for another to clarify the dynamics of a scene, and it often pertains to character attitude. For example, if you have said 'indignant' when you meant 'outraged', you can see the difference that it would make in the playing of the scene. Adjectives which are close in meaning can often alter entirely the character interaction. 'Confused' is not the same as 'disbelieving'; 'wry' is not the same as 'cynical', and so on. Tweaking an attitude with a change of adjective, or an extra word in the dialogue, can make a dead scene live. Maybe the attitudes are missing altogether; the scene is reading flatly because you wanted it played with a feeling of suppressed anger and hurt, but you didn't supply anything in the lead-up or the scene itself to suggest that.

Tweaking and polishing are fine-tuning processes, and you could go on forever changing attitudes and swapping lines. But sooner or later you have to step back and ask yourself if you have made *your intent* clear on the page. Have you ensured that whoever reads this is going to come to the same conclusions you did in the writing? If the answer is yes, then your script is ready.

13

Pre-production relationships

PRODUCER IS NOT A FOUR-LETTER WORD

You will have gleaned a little from Chapter 3 about how incredibly difficult it is to get a script made.

The most important, and yet most fragile, relationship a writer has, is with a producer. The producer may make only feature films, or only television drama, or both, depending on the market. You will be writing for either the big or small screen, depending on your idea. Unless the two of you come together in a symbiotic relationship, there is no production at the end of your work.

The fact that so many writers have bad experiences with producers is often their own fault. Just as you may have needed to research your script to be sure you've got it right, so you must research your producer.

Look at some Australian films that you have really enjoyed and make a note of the producer's name. If the same name crops up on three or more films, then put the name at the top of your list. Conversely, if you are given the name of a producer, check out the films or television drama this name appears on. If you hate everything, then scrap the name. Remember that in television you will need to be looking at the production company, or the executive producer, not the producer, for the latter is usually hired after the deal is cut and the programme is ready to move into pre-production.

When is a producer not a producer? When he/she is a line producer. When you check the producer's credits, make sure that these are not in fact 'line producer' credits. In film and television, the line producer handles the day-to-day production, the budget etc—*but is not the person responsible for making the deal which brings the project to production.* The same applies to associate producers, assistant producers and co-producers. They may be extremely skilled at their jobs, but you want the person who is capable of actually raising the pre-sale, dealing off-shore, and getting your script made.

So many times inexperienced writers will tell me they have a producer. Yet when I ask what this producer has produced, the answer is 'nothing yet'. This person is not a producer, but a would-be producer. Nor is this person a film and television producer if he/she has a video company which makes commercials or corporate videos.

The odds of a first-time producer getting the script of a first-time writer made are unbelievably low, and the reality is that experienced writers simply don't give their projects to producers without credits. So, breaking into producing is perhaps even harder than breaking into writing. It requires persistence, some source of finance, an unshakeable belief in yourself, an inability to take no for an answer and a love of doing deals.

In 1988 I decided I would move into producing with one of my own scripts. I had some funding from a film body and I was confident of making it all happen. Twelve months later I was broke, many tens of thousands of my own money down the drain. I was disillusioned and mentally broken and physically sick from batting my head against brick walls. I seemed permanently jetlagged, and my script was put into a bottom drawer and did not resurface until this year, when I did a rewrite and I'm now looking for a producer. What came out of this experience for me is an empathy with producers, an understanding of what they go through to bring a script to the screen.

It is true to say, as most writers complain, that producers are rarely creative. They may well not know a good script from a bad one, may not appreciate the subtlety of your creation, may not be able to explain why they like or dislike it. But all of that, while true, is irrelevant. They know whether they can sell it or not, thus getting it made, and that's what counts. There are a very small number of creative producers with fine instincts and the ability to discuss the nuances of your script with you, but they are a rare breed and difficult to find, since they often hibernate in faraway places for long periods.

Does it matter in the long run if your producer is creative? Unless you have written *The Piano* or something similar, probably not. Remember this, the audience isn't creative either. It knows nothing about the art of screenwriting. It simply wants to be entertained, and it knows what it likes. And the producer also knows what it likes. For my money, because I write for a mainstream audience, I'd rather have a producer who identified more closely with the audience than with me.

So, if a producer tells me, 'I hate the ending. I want the main character to come out on top because she's so strong and she shouldn't be a loser even for a moment,' it's a pretty safe bet that the audience is going to feel precisely the same way, and I'd better do something about the ending.

Never give a producer the rights to your script without at least one face-to-face meeting. And never sign any kind of agreement without having a solicitor who is familiar with these kinds of contracts look at it first. When you have a face-to-face meeting, don't be intimidated. Take a bold approach. Initiate the questioning. If the producer waxes lyrical about your script, ask why. Don't volunteer your own views, wait to hear what the producer says. If you come away thinking, 'This person doesn't even know what the script is about, and his/her ideas for casting stink,' then you can walk away with your script without having wasted too much time. If, on the other hand, the producer identifies the problems you knew were there but hoped no-one would notice; if the producer has clear-cut ideas on what should happen at the next draft, and you're surprised at how useful the suggestions are; if the producer has so much enthusiasm that you're starting to feel an adrenalin rush—then the chances are that you have found the right producer.

When it comes to the deal, we all tend to be blinded by the dollar signs, especially if we've been writing for months without a pennyworth of support. But very often the dollars don't make sense, and it's wise to look beyond the row of zeros to see what you're really letting yourself in for. Incidentally, if a producer offers you a deal which gives you no money up front whatsoever and asks you to defer all payments until a later date, steer a wide berth unless you have explored all other possibilities. I was offered a massive deferred fee by a producer to do a script in a hurry. I turned it down. A deferred fee is a 'maybe' fee. When he finally said in exasperation, 'What do I have to do to get you to write this script?' I replied, 'Put real money in my hand'. He did.

Let's assume that the deals being offered do carry a cash incentive. Here are two hypothetical examples of what to expect:

a) Casey Shonk has been producing for fifteen years. In that time he has produced eight films and one mini-series. Seven of the films were abysmal, one picked up several AFI awards (best cinematography, best music score, best art direction). The mini-series sold in twenty-three countries. That was four years ago. Casey loves your script, doesn't want to change a word, just cut the locations back a fraction to meet the budget. He's offering you a $10 000 option fee for a five-year option: $2000 up front and the rest at the end of the five years. What's more, he's prepared to pay you $100 000 for your script on the first day of principal photography, that is, when actual filming commences and give you 10 per cent of the producer's profits.

b) Peter Player was a director. He's been a producer for only four years. In that time he's had two very successful features which did well in Australia and even managed to find a small cinema audience overseas. He levels with you. The script needs another draft, and he doesn't have the money to pay for it. He's willing to take a twelve-month option for $1500 up front, with an extra twelve months at $2500. He'll make application to a film body for script development funding, all monies paid for drafts to be part of a total script fee of 3 per cent of the total budget (plus 5 per cent of producer's net profits). He wants to get a script editor to work with you, largely because the script doesn't exploit the visual possibilities, and he offers you several choices so that you won't feel uncomfortable.

Which deal do you take? You take b) and sign with Peter Player and then go out and celebrate. Why?

There are a number of clues as to the status of the two.

Casey has been around a long time. His last project was four years ago. He's a player on the way down.

Peter has made two acclaimed films in only four years. He's hot. A player on the way up.

Casey has a credit list which is nothing to brag about. He gets projects up, does the deal, but has a disaster to show for it. His AFI awards are in categories outside of his immediate control. At best his judgement is hit and miss, but he's obviously a great talker.

Peter has been a director. He has a visual eye. He knows how your script will look on the screen. Moreover, both of his productions have won both critical and audience acclaim.

'But Casey is offering more money, and more profits,' you say. Is he? Let's break down the deals. Casey will give you $2000.

You don't see any more money until the end of five years. During that time he may have dropped the project, gone bankrupt, or troppo, or all three. Peter is offering $1500 up front, and another $2500 in twelve months' time. At the end of two years you will have double the money from Peter that you would have received from Casey. What about the script fee? Casey is offering $100 000, a substantial amount. Peter is offering 3 per cent of the total budget. If the film costs $3 million, then you would only receive $90 000 and it appears you may be disadvantaged. But by the time your script is made, it's more likely that the budget would be $4–$5 million, so you would come out ahead.

Casey is offering 10 per cent of producer's net profits, Peter only 5 per cent. The reality of what's called a 'back end deal' is that the writer rarely sees any profits. This may well be, as it is in most cases, because there aren't any. Or it may simply be that it takes years to go into profit, everyone forgets about it, and you're certainly not going to fork out money for the auditing of the producer's accounts. Besides, from the little we know of these two producers, it's far more likely that Peter would pay you your profit share if there is any.

The last element which may be niggling away at you is that Peter wants you to work with a script editor.

THE SCRIPT EDITOR

Second only to the producer on the list of mythical monsters who are deadly enemies of the writer. Most writers I know are pathologically paranoid about working with an editor. I myself have the same fear, even though, when I'm not writing, I spend most of my time editing.

If you are a new writer you will be wondering what, precisely, a script editor does, and why you need one.

By definition, editing means cutting back, removing. In reality, a good script editor does far more than this. The Americans use the term script doctor; that is what the renowned Linda Segar (often called in to identify problems in major Hollywood scripts) is, and it's a term we should use here. I certainly call myself a script doctor. Most often we, as editors, are called in because the script is sick. It may have lost direction, it may be dying by degrees on the page, it almost certainly needs urgent medical attention. Our job is to make the script well, and that can't be achieved by simply cutting scenes or dialogue. Very often major surgery and several transplants are needed. But, just as there are good doctors and bad doctors, so there are good editors and bad ones. If you don't want your script killed by the wrong treatment, then you should interview the editor before you agree to embark on the edit. Ask the same kind of questions that you asked of the producer, and never accept a situation where you won't be working in a face-to-face situation with the editor. Your script will never be fixed to your satisfaction while you send rewrites across three states and get notes back. Some of the most exciting times I've had are when I sit with a writer and we're absolutely stumped on how to fix a problem, and one of us says, 'What if . . .?' and that becomes a springboard to a dozen new and fresh ideas that will enhance the script. When you interview an editor, these are the things you need to take on board and look for:

- A good editor protects your intent at all times.
- A good editor does not rewrite anything, but provides a variety of options so that you may rewrite.
- A good editor recognises what you were trying to say in the theme, or concept, and suggests ways of strengthening this.
- A good editor looks at the structure and identifies the spots where the spine is crooked, where the limbs have fallen off. With you, the editor explores different ways of restructuring so that the script will reach its maximum potential.
- A good editor will find a way of injecting an edge; a quirkiness; an individuality which makes the script more than it was before without adding anything to the actual volume of it. What's more, the editor will take no credit for this massive turnaround and will allow you to think it was entirely your own idea.
- A good editor will ask the pertinent questions of you which, when you work out the answers, will enable you to see where you went wrong.
- A good editor will know what you are trying to say even when you can't verbalise it.
- A good editor knows before you do when your characters lack motivation or are behaving according to your wants and not their own.
- A good editor may well be the best friend your script ever had. No script ever suffered from a good edit. Good scripts can be made great, bad scripts can be made workable if editors really know their trade.

Having said all that, I know of script editors who destroy scripts by imposing their own viewpoint; who offer no help other than to suggest swapping the dining room for the bedroom; who do maybe a total of ten hours work and take a $3000 fee; who completely destroy the writer's confidence. But these are in the minority. Likewise, there are a few great, mentor-like, editors. The rest fall somewhere in the middle, on various points of the graph.

You can see then why it's important that you have a say in the choice, rather than having the editor imposed upon you by the producer; for while the script editor's duty is to protect your intent, it's much harder to do this if the producer is footing the bill and has a different set of priorities for the script.

Often, if you're able to be objective enough, you can do a lot of doctoring on your own script. At the risk of making myself redundant, here are some of the tools I employ when working with writers, that you might try using on your own script.

DIY script editing

Whose story am I telling? This question is not the same as, 'Who is the character without whom the story cannot be told?' Often that will be the villain, the antagonist, but it isn't his story. The person whose story it is is the one who has the central experience, takes the journey, comes out changed. If that does not describe the central character in your script, then the focus is wrong.

What is the underpinning emotion or theme? Is it need, greed, loneliness, love, power, etc? Does this underpinning emotion relate to my central character? If it doesn't, then the chances are that your character is passive. It's true that the underpinning emotion or theme may be expressed by someone other than the main character. In *Wall Street* (20th Century Fox/Edward R. Pressman Prods 1988), that theme is greed. It's expressed by Michael Douglas, as the unscrupulous Gordon Gekko, when he utters the film's most memorable line: 'Greed is good'. But it is the Charlie Sheen character whose story it is (and who initially holds the same belief), who makes the journey and learns that greed is not good.

Why should anyone pay $11–$12 to see this film? You'll know from your answer to this one whether you are being self-indulgent. You may have a lot of reasons, but unless one of them is, 'Because it's a bloody good yarn,' and that's irrespective of genre, you need to go back to the drawing board. *The Piano* is a bloody good yarn. So is *Crocodile Dundee*. These films have totally different audience demographics but, in each case, the audience expectations were met. They got their money's worth.

What do I want the audience to take away from this film? Once you verbalise this thought you will know what it is you are trying to express through your script. You will then be able to go back to the script and see if you actually conveyed it.

Why? This is probably a good script doctor's favourite word, and you can ask it of every element of your script. Why is he saying that? Why is she in this scene? Why do they argue? Why didn't they call the police? If you have no reasonable answer, then you've probably got a problem.

Momentum and structure repair

You know that your script has lost momentum. It suddenly seems flat and static, but you can't pinpoint where it happened and you don't know how to fix it. Follow this series of steps:

Designate each scene which contains a plot point. Mark it PD for plot driven. Remember, this plot point must not simply be a reiteration of what has previously been established for audience and characters. If you aren't sure yourself, take the conservative approach and don't mark the scene. Keep a list of the scene numbers on a separate sheet under the PD heading.

Now do the same thing with each scene that is character driven. Remember, once again, that the scene should progress the character, or tell us, or another character something that we didn't already know. Perhaps even the main character was unaware of this element. As before, if it isn't clear, don't mark it. List these scene numbers alongside your others under the heading CD. Some scenes will be both plot and character driven. Put them in both lists. Once you do this you'll see at a glance where you suddenly have a big jump, from say, scene 63 to scene 79. There could be as much as sixteen minutes of screen time where the audience is being told nothing new whatsoever and the script has stopped dead in its tracks. Once you identify the problem, you then need to create either some progressive plot points or character development for that area. Often you can actually rearrange some of your scenes, or take content from one scene that is very full of plot and character points, and inject some of those points into the area that has come to a halt. Alternatively, there's every chance that you can cut a lot of those scenes which are neither plot nor character driven.

Checking character function

It's fair to say that if two characters share the same viewpoint, the same attitudes, the same wants and needs, one of them is redundant. Sometimes though, you have an interesting character whom you just can't make work.

Here's one way to check if a character is actually doing something.

Make a diagram, as below, with your characters' names set around a clock face. Your lead should be at twelve o'clock, your antagonist at six o'clock. The position of the rest is not really important. Now, starting with twelve o'clock, your main character, draw a line from that name to the name of every character with whom there is real interaction. Continue around the clock. You'll get a diagram something like this:

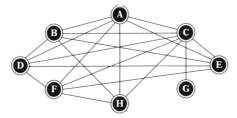

If you have one character that is disconnected from the rest, or perhaps has only a tenuous connection to one other, then reread everything you have given that character. There's every chance the character has no function and you can write it out.

Peaks and troughs

Very often, especially in a script with a lot of plot, the script will hit a high point (peak) and then slump afterwards (trough). This means that the audience attention slides and it has to work doubly hard to climb out of the trough to make it to the next peak with you.

A graph of such a script may look something like this:

a)

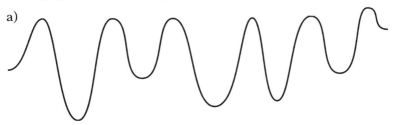

You can see from the wave effect how far we have to travel from the bottom of the trough to the top of the peak. Now it is essential to rest an audience. You can't just hammer at them for 90–120 minutes without ever giving them breathing space. They also need that time to assimilate and evaluate the information they are being given, just as the characters do, especially if your screenplay is a shared experience requiring subjective involvement from the audience that you cannot afford to lose. So what you may need to do is lower the peaks a little, but raise the troughs to plateaus. I call this 'terraced dynamics', which is a term generally used in music. Now your graph might look like this:

b)

Here you can see that the script is always ascending, with the exception of a small trough after your first peak. Often that's inevitable. You've used a moment, a hook, to grab the audience, but now you are into the set-up, and until the audience starts to relate and empathise, their interest will slide a little.

How do you introduce terraced dynamics? You do it by maintaining the tension, conflict and thrust of the peak into the scenes that follow. If you go from a huge moment of terror or action, for example (peak), and cut straight into a love scene between two people who weren't involved in the peak, then you plunge instantly into a trough. But if you carry the mood, the attitudes and the tension from the peak across the following scenes, letting go of them only slowly, then you will plateau out and maintain the momentum until you start to accelerate towards the next peak.

These exercises look easy on paper, but it's recognising the problems in the first place that is difficult. Remember, once your script is into shooting, it is no longer your baby. It has a life of its own. At this stage of its development though, you may feel like Sally, a single parent with nowhere to turn for help. The right producer and script editor can supply all the support you need.

14

The television serial

WRITING 'SOAP' WITHOUT GETTING YOUR HANDS DIRTY

Formula television writing is hard to break into, and even harder to break away from once you're there. Many new writers hold serial writing in contempt, but the fact remains that almost all of our most respected screenwriters have done stints on a soap at some time or another. By soap, I mean any long-term formula drama series. It's an extremely lucrative form of writing and often pays the bills and provides security when you're facing creative block, or your pet project just won't get off the ground. It has both advantages and disadvantages and you must take both on board and weigh them up carefully before you make a decision.

The advantages are:

1 *Financial security.* I don't know of any other writing form which allows you to make so much money, so quickly, for so little work. How much money are we talking here? Well, a half-hour serial episode, depending on where it's being shown, and whether you supply your own scene breakdown, etc, will pay you something between $2500–$6000. This is for a script of approximately 24 pages which will take you somewhere between two days and two weeks to write. If the producers like your work, you can expect to get a script about every four to five weeks; or you may get an entire block, five episodes in a row, about every eight weeks or so.

2 *Brain rejuvenation.* Whilst it's an exaggeration to say that you

can write a serial with your eyes closed, you can get to a stage where you know the format, the formula, and the characters so well that the writing becomes second nature, with no brain drain at all. If you've come from working on a number of your own screenplays where the creative juices have been working overtime, and your brain feels like it's been run over by an entire convoy of trucks, then serial writing can be like a six-month stay at a rehabilitation hospital where they pay you to get better. It's never your craft skills that are affected by brain drain, only your creative forces, so you can still write, as long as someone tells you what you're writing about.

3   *Credit.* The only way you are going to be considered a professional writer (as opposed to a good or bad one) is to have a credit on a major production. The serial is often the quickest way for a new writer to make that official transition from amateur status to professional.

4   *Experience and discipline.* You'll learn a lot about how to write, and how not to write, from working on a soap. You will have certain things imposed upon you which you will have to adapt to, and you will face the discipline of writing to a specific length in a specific amount of time. Since most writers lack discipline, this in itself is a valuable lesson which you can take away with you once you go freelance again. I learned through my years with Grundy's the discipline of writing ten pages of script a day. It was the only way I could fit in working with the storyliners, creating the characters, writing the 'majors' (individual stories), attending script meetings, and so on and so forth. I still, now (when I'm serious about a project and not just dabbling), write ten pages of script a day. This means that I can do a complete screenplay in ten days or so. Of course I then follow my own rules, put it away, and do rewrites on my first draft. However, I have a reputation for being a fast writer, and that discipline has provided me with four lucrative commissioned scripts, paid for by the producers, over the past two years which have kept me solvent while I worked on my own projects.

5   *Reputation.* Producers and story editors tend to move from show to show. If you establish yourself as a quality writer who hits the mark and brings the script in to length and on deadline, your name will stay with them when they move to another show, and you'll find yourself on their writing list. You build a reputation this way, and it isn't unusual for a

good serial writer to be writing for several different shows, with different production companies and on different networks. I know of one serial writer who bought a house with a twenty-five year mortgage and paid it off in four years.

So why doesn't everybody race out and become serial writers? For one thing, it isn't that easy to get in, to get started. More than that, though, there's an element of being an employee, of working nine to five, that some people can't tolerate. Those of us who are writers in our souls, who would write not for the money but for the sheer exhilaration of it, need our space, our freedom. There are more tangible problems.

The disadvantages are:

1 *Financial security.* The dream of this may have got you into serial writing in the first place, but it can become the nightmare that keeps you there, imprisoned. Once you start to make big money doing formula writing, you promise yourself that you'll do a few more episodes, then throw it in and devote the time to your own projects. The trouble is, you never do. It requires amazing fortitude to just say no to perhaps several thousand dollars a week and go back to not knowing how you're going to make the car payment next month. Most of us can't do it consciously, and I don't know of any writer that has successfully written a terrific 'spec' film script for themselves at the same time as being heavily into writing formula television. What we do instead is subconsciously engineer our own demise. We turn in a few dodgy scripts until we finally get dropped from the show. We then have someone to blame when we no longer have the big money coming in. I took more and more liberties with Grundy's, engineering a showdown which would give me my freedom, because I didn't have the guts to say no to the money. I know many other writers who've done the same thing, though not perhaps to the same extreme. So, be aware that the money can be a trap, and that you might never write the screenplay you dream of. You'll be too busy checking your bank balance.

2 *Stifled creativity.* You will be writing stories someone else created, for characters someone else created. The role of the serial writer is interpretive rather than creative. This is a fact, and it's definitely the downside. Some serials are structured so rigidly that the scene breakdown has to be followed exactly, and it will even tell you that 'Wayne tells Tiffany that

. . .' I call it join-the-dots writing. Much like the puzzles we used to do as kids, everything is there on the page in 'dot' form; all you have to do is join them up to see what the picture is. The whole idea of writing serial television is consistency and uniformity. Basically the ideal situation is for all the scripts to look as though they've been written by the one person.

Perhaps you don't feel confident enough to plunge straight into a screenplay. Or maybe you want to write, but original stories are not your forte. Let's simply assume that you've made the decision to write soap. How do you go about it? The first thing to do is decide what you want your function to be. If you want to write episodes, then target the show and watch it carefully for four to six weeks, so that you have a reasonable idea of how it's structured and who the major characters are. Next, look at the end credits and discover the name of the script producer or, if there isn't one, the story editor. Phone the production company and speak to this person by name. Enthuse about the show, tell a little of what you've done (embroider the truth rather than lie outright) and ask if you can do a writer's submission.

Submissions are like entrance exams for unknown writers. You are given a script to read, and then the following episode's storyline or scene breakdown and asked to write (generally) one segment. The producer, script producer, story editor or chief script editor will then read what you have submitted and decide if your style suits the show. Remember, you're not trying to impress them with your originality, you are trying to write as closely to the style of the other script, and all the episodes you have seen, as you possibly can. *Never* ask to do a submission on a show that you haven't watched.

It may be that you don't want to make the writers' list, but are interested in some other function. The way in is to become a trainee storyliner, and that requires simply applying to the production company and hassling them until a vacancy comes up. From there you can start to work your way up through the script department. Let's look at the various functions involved, and how they fit in the team:

Script producer/story editor: Script producer is a relatively new position, and not all shows have them. Primarily, the function of whoever is heading the script department is to come up with the content, that is, create all the stories and the characters for the show. This person, regardless of title, will also supervise the writers and train the storyliners, liaise with the script editors and the producer, and may also, with the production company's trust, create the style for the show. This was my job on *Prisoner*, and I was also head writer. My title was story editor, since 'script producer' didn't exist at that time. Where there is a script producer, the story editor will most likely be responsible for development of the stories and characters that have been created.

The storyliners meet with the story editor, and often the writers. From the stories and characters available for any given block of episodes, storylines are created, high points manufactured, cliffhangers discussed. Smooth transitions or marrying of stories are brought about. Particular attention has to be paid to which actors may be used in any given episode; what locations are available, by how much night shooting is going to infringe on the production schedule and so on and so forth. The storyliners then will either type up a complete storyline from which the writer will create a scene breakdown, or will, in most cases, provide a ready-made, join-the-dots, scene breakdown. You will take that away as the writer and complete your script to its requirements. Your completed script will then go to the script editor. The script editor's function is to see that you have conformed to the formula; that you have not imposed speech patterns or attitudes that are alien to the way the characters have been set up; that you haven't used additional locations or cast which are not covered in the budget; and that your scenes run to the times that you claim they do, so that your script won't be over or under time. It's a very different function to script editing a feature film.

The hierarchy diagram might look something like this:

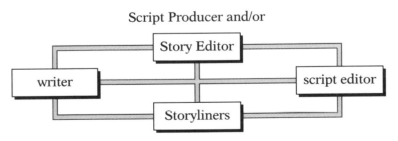

Script Producer and/or Story Editor — writer — script editor — Storyliners

You will notice that the producer's name is not here. Whilst the producer will liaise closely with the script producer and/or story editor, that's generally where the involvement in the writing side ends. The sheer logistics of controlling two hours of television every week (which is equivalent to a feature film) along with staff, cast, directors, etc, leaves very little time for hands-on involvement in the creative process, although most producers do read all scripts.

You will find when you get your first script that there is a set amount of stock, or regular, permanent sets, and a small allowance for guest sets (a set which is not going to be used again). Similarly, there is an allocation for outside broadcast, or location. This is limited because, of course, it takes far longer to transport cast and crew to a location, set up, and then shoot, than it does to shoot in the studio with a set that is permanently erected. So don't ever decide that the scene in the milk bar would look better out on the beach without checking very carefully that the beach is already a designated location for that block of episodes, and without passing your idea past the story editor or head storyliner.

Also, don't make a judgement (or, if you do, don't verbalise it) that the scene breakdown is crappy and you'd much rather rewrite the whole thing before you start your script. Storylining is not an easy job if it's done well, and many storyliners are brain dead by Friday afternoons. They don't appreciate hearing that what they've written is crap. Rather, take the approach that you are having problems with it and would appreciate it if you could swap scenes 3 and 7 (or whatever) and move 5 to the bedroom which is a stock set that you're using in scene 11. Very few story editors or storyliners will say no if they can see the logic, but you must make the right approach.

Your relationship with the script editor is of utmost importance. More than anyone else, a script editor can have a writer dropped from the writers' list if there's antagonism between them, or if the writer is causing genuine grief to the editor. The way to cause a serial script editor genuine grief is to write double what you've been asked to; write far less than the time required so that the script editor has to create a lot more content rather than cut it back; forget the follow-throughs from the previous episode (those attitudes or plot points that have already been set up but which the writer must maintain through the characters); time your scenes completely wrongly.

Timing the scene

Your script editor uses a stopwatch, and you will need one too. The second hand on your watch won't suffice.

Your scenes are divided into action—'big print'—and dialogue. Before you time the scene, read it quickly twice, so that you know what's in your big print and who is speaking in your dialogue. Take on board whether it's a confrontational scene, say an argument, in which the dialogue is faster than usual, and which of the regular characters is in it and what their speech rates are. Now, knowing what is in the big print, start timing the scene without reading the big print (action) but visualising it in your head. So, if it says, 'Wayne walks from the car to the front door, he stops and takes a rose from the garden,' that's going to take longer to play than it does to read, and you're timing how long it plays. Don't time anything in the big print that doesn't take up time on the screen (clothes, or a prop, for example, are seen instantly). Remember, you're concerned with how much screen time this scene needs, not how long it takes you to read it.

One of the editors I worked with for a long time used to use two fingers for the legs of the character. I'd often see him with the stop watch in one hand and his two fingers walking, sometimes running, across his desk top as he mouthed silently to himself.

Your timing is rounded off to the nearest five seconds, but it needs to be accurate. Let's say you were out by five seconds a scene, over twenty-four scenes. You'd be two minutes out on the episode. Then, if the script editor's timings proved you were out another five seconds on half the scenes, three minutes would be the total either lost or gained. Timing isn't a mystery sent to haunt writers. It's simply a craft skill like all the others we've talked about. It can be learned and mastered with practice. So, if you seriously want to work in television, buy a stopwatch and start practising.

Making your own mark

Whilst I have said that one of the drawbacks is the feeling of merely joining the dots, the skilled serial writer can still make an impact by exploiting those areas which are not necessarily predetermined. Let's go back to the scene where you're told, 'Wayne tells Tiffany that . . .' Let's say he's telling her that he likes her, and he's been wanting to ask her out. Let's say the scene is in Wayne's mum's kitchen. Those are the predetermined elements that you can't do anything about. You must use the location, and you must establish certain things in the dialogue.

Other than that, though, you can be imaginative. Use the action. Play that against the dialogue. Maybe Wayne is trying to impress Tiffany by making her coffee. Maybe he's making an awful mess of it because he's nervous and she's having trouble keeping a straight face. Perhaps he puts fourteen teaspoons of sugar in her cup without realising. She's watching but can't interrupt his carefully prepared speech. Maybe he gets his words all wrong and she doesn't understand what he's trying to say to her. Provided you do not go against the grain of the characters, nor the point of the scene, you have carte blanche to turn this banal exchange into exciting romantic comedy, remembering the demographic of the audience and what they will relate to. The good serial writer uses what's available, and those little gems of scenes are often what lifts the pace and the feel of the episode above the ordinary. Don't go overboard. Serials are played naturalistically, even though storylines can be melodramatic, but stretch the scene (in scope, not length) beyond the parameters you have been given. You'll find you get a lot more scripts that way.

Two more things. Like the characters you're writing for, even if this is not a show you would normally watch. Get caught up in their lives and care where their stories are going. You'll never be happy writing them otherwise. And remember, creating that much drama content per week has to be a team effort. When you look at the logistics of making the equivalent of a feature film every seven days, the wonder is not that it's bad, but that it ever happens at all.

15

Selling your script

TO MARKET, TO MARKET . . .

By now, you have a first-draft script which you honestly believe is as good as you can get it. Now what do you do with it? If your intention is to see it made into a film, or a television series, even if it be ten years down the track, then you must get it out to the marketplace. The purpose of this chapter is to streamline that process with as little cost to you as possible.

The finished script

Your script will now consist of somewhere between 90 and 125 pages. It will be printed on one side of the paper only, using the format we talked about earlier. You will not have written anything on it in either pen or pencil, and the pages will all be numbered in the top right-hand corner. Moreover, the front page (unnumbered) will carry not only the title, and your writing credit, but a copyright symbol and your full name and address in the bottom left-hand corner. You are ready to take it to the printer. If you can afford a cover with some specific design or artwork, or a photograph which suggests the nature of your subject matter, then by all means go ahead and get one. But remember this. A bad script is never sold just because it has a nice cover, and a good script isn't hindered by not having one.

Depending upon the graphics capability of your computer, you can perhaps do some fancy design incorporating your title which will print quite well onto plain white card for your cover.

More often than not, a simple clear sheet of acetate, through which your front page can be seen, will do the job quite adequately.

I tend to go to my local office equipment and stationery supply shop and buy comb binders and a packet of textured-card A4 covers in the same colour as the binders. I then use either a gold or silver fine artline pen to italicise my title by hand. Royal blue covers with matching comb binders (or grey with grey) and discreet silver lettering can look pretty snazzy, and it actually costs me less than if I asked the printer to use black combs and clear acetate, with a plain white card back cover.

Your scripts should always be comb-bound if possible, and choose a comb which is just slightly larger than the script itself. This will allow readers to turn pages easily and, one hopes, when you get your script back it will still be in good enough shape to send out to someone else. Bind it any other way and you'll probably find yourself throwing it out. A script can come back from one reader (a film office, a producer) looking like fifty people have handled it. When you send it out the next time, you're at a psychological disadvantage, for the new reader will think it's already been through dozens of hands and rejected.

If you can afford to have your covers laminated, then do so. It will prolong the life of your script. Also, never send out a script with a front page showing a copyright date that is more than two years old. Update your front page frequently, changing the date. Your copyright is always protected from the date of your first writing of the material. Any photocopy shop will replace your front page for about 50 cents.

I've mentioned the printer earlier in this chapter, but of course I'm not suggesting that you go somewhere and have your entire script typeset and printed. High quality photocopying is all that's necessary. You'll need at least six copies, and you can expect to pay, all up, anywhere between $12 and $20 per copy. Be prepared to leave the script at the printers overnight to ensure a good job. And always check that the numbered pages have been bound in the right order, and up the right way.

Now you're ready to take on the world, but you just don't send out scripts indiscriminately. You need a game plan.

Where to send it

One of the major complaints I hear from new writers is that they don't know where to send their work. How will they get to a producer? Who do they talk to at the film office? A million and one whinges to which I have but one reply. Find out! No-one is going to hold your hand. No-one is going to make it easy for you. Screenwriting as a career is highly competitive, and it's also isolated and insular. Writers don't often get together and help each other. It's mostly a matter of self-preservation, since there is so little work, and so many writers competing for it.

The *Encore Directory* a Reed Business Publishing P/L Publication can be your best friend at this stage. It is an annual professional film makers directory which lists film personnel in all areas. It is not available in shops, but can be ordered from its Sydney distributor by phone. Directory Assistance at Telecom will have a current number. You, as a new writer, will be able to find, in a well laid-out, cross referenced format, the names of producers, directors, script editors, writers' agents, film solicitors, state film funding bodies, film distributors, television networks and so on. In fact, everything you always wanted to know but didn't know who to ask.

Not only will you get the names and addresses you need, but you'll get a fair indication from the credits listed whether you're targeting a person who will be receptive to your work. Let's look at the list and see who may be useful to you and what your approach might be to each:

Agents

There are writers who are rightly suspicious of agents, seeing them as grasping ten per cent of everything, when they have been given a perfect script which could sell itself. Others work in television production areas where their employment is ongoing, and so they see no necessity for an agent. I must admit that I never had an agent until a year ago. And this past year has been the most rewarding of the last ten. The reality is, if you're serious about writing as a career, sooner or later you need someone to act for you.

If you are lucky enough to have a good agent, you then have someone who believes in your work and your talent, who will do a lot of the messy work for you. Moreover, your agent, if he/she has a good reputation, is able to reach producers who may not respond to you personally. Once the agent gets a producer to look at your script, the producer will respond freely to the agent, giving a reaction that you may not be privy to. The producer's response to you (assuming you can get one to read your script) could be a polite 'no', praising your script but saying it's not what they're looking for. A standard diplomatic brushoff. However, the response to the agent will most likely comment on *why* there's been a negative reaction (your agent will push for a reason) and what particular areas don't work. You'll at least know what you need to do next.

So, how do you get an agent? Well, you don't simply send an unsolicited script with a covering letter saying you want the agent to act for you. If you can bring yourself to do it, you make an introductory phone call to break the ice, and ask for ten minutes so that you can meet. At that meeting you sell yourself—why you want to write, what you have to say, whom you're writing for, why the agent should handle you—without being over-egotistical. If you impress the agent enough, you will at least get your script read, and that in turn may lead to the agent agreeing to take you on as a client. If you can't get a meeting, then you politely press for the agent to read your script and give you some feedback, hoping for the same result.

Most of us can't bring ourselves to make that initial phone call, however. It's simply too difficult to say, 'You don't know me but . . .' What I suggest then is not a letter but a fax. (A letter can be ignored, but no-one can pretend they didn't receive a fax.) The fax can be sent from a post office, should be addressed to the agent you're courting personally, not just to the company, and is designed to pique their interest, so it might read something like this:

Dear . . .

As a new writer, anxious to go places as quickly as possible, I'm seeking professional representation.

Currently I have two great projects ready for the market place.

'A' (title) is a broad-spectrum action adventure about an Aboriginal test pilot in conflict with his family for defying tradition . . . sort of a Top Gun meets The Fringe Dwellers.

'B' is a low-budget thriller packed with tension and with several unique twists. It would adapt well as a telemovie.

May I impose upon you to look at my work, with a view to your acting for me? I wouldn't be asking if I did not believe I was ready. Perhaps you would spare me a few minutes of your time. Lunch is beyond my means at present, but maybe we could 'do coffee'.

Etc, etc.

Keep the tone chatty but professional, with a light touch, and remember to add your full name and address. Try not to let any of your doubts or neuroses creep in. An agent who believes in you will back you to the hilt, and give you support and encouragement when needed, but doesn't want to act as your shrink or your mother. Any suggestion from the outset that you're going to be a proverbial pain in the bum may well put the agent off before your work is even looked at.

Australian Film Commission

Known as the AFC, this is our national body for the support of the film and television industry. For a new writer, the AFC, or any of the state film funding bodies, can be of invaluable help. All provide script development funding, which gives you a livable amount of money while you write the next draft of your script. The guidelines are similar for all film bodies and I'll talk in detail about making an application later in this chapter.

Australian Writers Guild

The guild is an organisation set up for the support of professional writers. In many ways it functions as a union, negotiating award rates for writers on various television shows, creating standard contracts and option agreements, arbitrating when disputes arise. Whilst you will not be eligible for full membership if you don't have any professional writing credits, you can certainly become an associate member which entitles you to pretty much everything full membership confers except voting rights, or the right to stand for election. The AWG is useful to new members in four ways. Firstly, it supplies a regular bulletin, *Viewpoint*, which allows you to see the issues confronting professional writers, and which also provides useful articles and information about openings in the market. Secondly, each state has its own committee which has regular monthly meetings and irregular social gatherings. You will be welcomed at both as an associate member, and it will give you a chance to meet with others who have either successfully weathered the transition to professional, or are still trying to. Thirdly, it provides each member with a script assessment service for a nominal fee. This means that if you aren't sure whether your script is ready for a producer, or a film funding application, you can get professional feedback from an experienced writer which may well be invaluable to you.

Last on the list is the advice available on contracts, options, minimum fees, how to negotiate and so on and so forth. It isn't cheap to join, but it may well be a worthwhile investment for you.

Directors

Many new writers believe that if they get their project to a director who likes it, the director will take up the cause and get the script into production. It's often true in Hollywood, but it simply doesn't work that way here. Most directors are for hire. Producers offer them projects and the directors accept or decline. There are a few 'name' directors who would be capable of initiating production, but they spend most of their time out of the country and, in any case, have agents who make it difficult to approach them. However, if you happen to find yourself sitting next to Peter Weir or Gillian Armstrong in a captive situation, by all means tell them about your script. You never know . . . stranger things have happened.

Distributors

These people do deals on films, they don't act as mentors for writers. Most distributors will not look at scripts even from experienced writers unless there's a package presented by a producer. This means that the producer presents your script, plus a budget, proposed lead actors and director. Don't waste time and money sending an unsolicited script. The chances of it being read, or even returned, are pretty remote.

(Australian) Film Financing Corporation

Although this is a government body, and is involved in the production of most of our film and television projects, it does not give out grants, it does not give assessments, it does not find you a producer. In fact, it really doesn't deal with writers per se at all, so don't confuse it with the AFC or any of the other film funding bodies. It functions along the same lines as a merchant bank, and its major criterion for investment is commercial viability.

Producers

Whether you like the idea or not, a producer who genuinely likes your script is your best chance of getting it made. We've talked at length about the writer/producer relationship, but I would add this. Break the ice with the same kind of approach that you might make to a targeted agent. Then send a one page 'pitch' of your script. If the producer responds that the genre is of no interest, or their project file already has three similar scripts, you won't have wasted time and money sending a script. Once you have some kind of response, you've established a relationship with that producer and can more easily offer your next project. I have a terrific relationship with a major producer which has been going on for eighteen months. We send each other lots of rude faxes—I call him the Phantom, he calls me Banana Bandit—and we like each other a lot, even though we've only met twice. We're still negotiating a contract on one project, but the point is that we have enough rapport that I can pitch any idea to him and get a genuine response. We also now know enough about each other to know we'd be comfortable working together.

Production companies

If you want to target Grundy's, or Crawford's, or Simpson Le Mesurier, or JNP or even one of the lesser television production companies, again, do not send an unsolicited script. Make a phone call and ask who their head of creative development is. Get a name, and make sure you know how to spell it. This is the person who'll be looking at your script. Again, make contact either by fax or phone and 'pitch' the idea. Don't send the full script until they agree to read it.

State film bodies

See everything listed earlier for *Australian Film Commission*. Each State has one and they are not hard to approach. Whether you get any money out of them is another matter entirely, but hopefully the section following later in this chapter on applications will, I hope, help you to maximise your chances.

Television networks

Each network has a drama department, and a head of that department. Again, don't send an unsolicited script until you know what they might be looking for. Still, people like Bevan Lee (Nine Network) are approachable, charming, and helpful, and will brush you off in the nicest possible manner if you have nothing they're interested in, and encourage you if there's even a chance you've got something new and commercial. Even here though, your best chance of success is to go through a reputable producer, and each network has producers whom they prefer dealing with. The ABC, in both Sydney and Melbourne, has commissioning editors in its drama departments and they will look at material without producers attached, but it's still wise to make contact first. If you live in Townsville or Broome, be very conscious that network drama decisions still come out of Sydney or Melbourne, despite the fact that one of the most prolific film and television production companies in the country, Barron Films, is situated in Perth.

Let's assume now that you've decided you want to take three months to really rework your script before you send it to the producer of your choice. It's a sensible idea, because if you get a negative reaction to it the first time, the producer will most likely be unwilling to read it again. So how do you live while you do this work? That's where film offices come in.

Making an application for funding

The first thing to familiarise yourself with is your local State film office, whether it be the New South Wales Film and Television Office, Film Victoria, Film Queensland, and so on. Once again, you'll find them listed in *Encore* or you can phone your State government arts department and ask for information. And, wherever you live, you can make an application to the AFC.

You start by calling up, asking the name of the project officer for script development, and then ask to be sent their guidelines and an application form. You may also go in and talk to the project officer about your script. That's what they're there for. Generally script development project officers are writers who are taking a break from writing. The turnover in any film office is usually between six months and three years. Occasionally you'll cop a public servant who knows little or nothing about scripts, and you just have to wear it. The project officer is not the one who decides whether you get funding or not.

You will find that different rules apply for uncredited writers than for credited ones. A professional, i.e. credited, writer may submit a treatment of a proposed script and ask for funding to write the first draft. A new writer, however, will have to submit a completed first draft and ask for funding to do the rewrite. Many vocal new writers, associate members of the Australian Writers Guild, scream long and loud about this being unfair and discriminatory. On the contrary, it makes perfect sense. A seasoned writer has already proven a knowledge of structure, dialogue, formatting, etc, etc, in former scripts. That writer comes with those craft skills as part of his or her equipment. The new writer, on the other hand, may fluke it for a treatment, and have a really good story, but have none of the craft skills and be incapable of turning it into a script. I assess and edit for two film offices and, before the prerequisite was changed, I can't tell you how many terrific treatments made diabolical scripts, if indeed they made anything resembling a script at all. So, accept that you are going to have to write the first draft off your own bat, without financial support. Nothing will stop you anyway if you really want to write, and funding from a film body isn't a right, it's a privilege.

Next you must make an application which ranges in form from a letter plus a development budget for the New South Wales Film and Television Office, to a tome resembling an interrogation book, with a JP's witnessing of your signature required for Film Queensland. This can be daunting, but if you read the material carefully, it's not impossible. If a particular section does not apply to you, simply write 'Not Applicable' or 'Not Known'. The monster that looms in every application, however, is the development budget. Nine out of ten that I see are filled out incorrectly.

The chart below is a sample budget which we'll look at in detail. Remember, it is not the budget of your film. It is the budget of the development of your script.

	Applicant's contribution		Film Office contribution	
	cash	deferred	previous	requested
Option				
Treatment		$5000		
1st draft		$10 000		
2nd draft				$10 000
3rd draft				
Script Ed.				$3000
Research	$500			
Producer				
Typing and Copying	$250			$ 250
Marketing				
TOTALS	$750	$15 000		$13 250

Total development budget $29 000

Big Screen, Small Screen

You are asking a film office to give you $13 250, $3000 of which you would give to a script editor (which would probably be a prerequisite for a new writer, and the editor would have to be approved), and yet your total budget comes to $29 000. Why? The amounts listed on the left-hand side of the page under *Applicant's contribution* is deemed to be your investment in your own work. That investment can be cash, money you have laid out for research, or an independent assessment, or photocopying, or a script editor. The rest of your equity in your script is in the form of deferrals. A deferment or deferral is an amount you would have paid yourself at market rates for the work completed, but have agreed not to. It can only be applied to work completed, so if you're asking for second-draft funding, then you can't put amounts for third draft, producer's fees and so on in your deferred column. When you add up your totals, you want figures which show that you will have just as big, if not bigger, an investment in your script as the film office does. Investment is the key word, for no film office gives grants, contrary to what many writers believe. A grant is non-repayable, and literary boards and arts councils give grants in all areas of the arts, but not usually film. The investment a film office makes is in the production of your project. So, it gives you money to write your script, but it expects that money to be paid back, with extremely high interest, if your script is ever produced. This freaks out some new writers when they actually read the contract, especially those who believed they were getting a grant. The reality is that you, as the writer, don't ever actually make the repayment, or pay the interest. If you never sell your script, you keep the money, and it's even possible that you won't pay tax on it (check it out) because it is a loan, not a grant. If a producer buys your script he or she takes over the repayment responsibility. And while some producers might deduct the capital amount from your writer's fees, he or she is responsible for the interest, and for the profit points that the film office might require in your project. So don't let the contract scare you. Film offices are there to help. However, be very aware that your project's funding will depend upon assessments by two assessors, one generally a writer, one usually a producer. If one assessment is positive, the other negative, a third is called for. As much as we assessors try to be objective and unbiased, it's very difficult to ignore personal preferences. So, if I'm assessing an action cop movie, I have to work doubly hard at forgetting that I don't like the genre, and simply let the script stand or fall on its merits.

If you get a knockback, don't be afraid to submit your next script. A knockback doesn't necessarily mean that you can't write, only that this script doesn't readily meet the market, or the current guidelines.

Film Queensland and the New South Wales Film and Television Office have separate schemes for funding new writers and it's worth enquiring about them.

So, there's little more I can tell you except to go out there and do it. Ultimately, three things count—the right contact, the right timing, and the right script. Often one of these elements will be missing. Then you have to compensate by being more flexible, more dynamic, more diligent. Writing a script is one thing, getting it made is another. In the end, the only person who can sell your script is YOU.

Film and television references

Arcade (TV) A Network Ten Production 1980
Producer: Peter Barnados
Writer: Various
Director: Various

Alien (Film) 20th Century Fox 1979
Producer: Gordon Carroll/David Giler/Walter Hill
Writer: Dan O'Bannon
Director: Ridley Scott

Basic Instinct (Film) Caralco/Le Studio Canal 1992
Producer: Alan Marshall
Writer: Joe Esztherhas
Director: Paul Verhoeven

The Big Chill (Film) Columbia/Carson Prods Group Ltd 1983
Producer: Michael Shamberg
Writer: Lawrence Kasdan/Barbara Benedek
Director: Lawrence Kasdan

The Big Steal (Film) Cascade Films/Hoyts/AFFC 1990
Producer: Nadia Tass and David Parker
Writer: David Parker
Director: Nadia Tass

The Breakfast Club (Film) Universal/A & M Films 1985
Producer: Ned Tanen/John Hughes
Writer: John Hughes
Director: John Hughes

Cathy Come Home (TV) Granada Television 1966
Producer/writer/director: Ken Loach

Chaplin (Film) Caralco/Le Studio Canal 1992
Producer: Richard Attenborough/Mario Kassar
Writer: William Boyd/Bryan Forbes/William Goldman
Director: Richard Attenborough

A Country Practice (TV) JNP Productions 1983–
Executive Producer: James Davern
Writers/producers/directors: Various

Crocodile Dundee (Film) Hoyts/Rimfire Films 1986
Producer: John Cornell
Writer: Paul Hogan/Ken Shadie
Director: Peter Faiman

Division Four (TV) Crawford Productions late '60s–early '70s
Executive Producer: Hector Crawford
Producers/writers/directors: Various

Driving Miss Daisy (Film) Majestic Films/Warner Bros 1990
Producer: Richard D. Zanuck/Lili Fini Zanuck
Writer: Alfred Uhry
Director: Bruce Beresford

ET: The Extraterrestrial (Film) Universal 1982
Producer: Steven Spielberg/Kathleen Kennedy
Writer: Melissa Mathison
Director: Steven Spielberg

Falling in Love (Film) Paramount/Marvin Worth Prods 1984
Producer: Marvin Worth
Writer: Michael Christofer
Director: Ulu Grosbard

Fawlty Towers (TV) BBC Enterprises 1978–79
Producer: Douglas Argent/Bob Spiers
Writer: John Cleese/Connie Booth
Director: John Howard Davies

Flirting (Film) Kennedy Miller/Warner Bros 1990
Producer: George Miller/Doug Mitchell/Terry Hayes
Writer: John Duigan
Director: John Duigan

Fran (Film) Barron Films 1985
Producer: David Rapsey
Writer: Glenda Hambly
Director: Glenda Hambly

The Fugitive (TV) Quinn Martin Productions 1963–67
Executive Producer: Quinn Martin
Producers/writers/directors: Various

Ginger Meggs (Film) John Sexton Productions/Hoyts

Producer: John Sexton
Writer: Michael Latimer
Director: Jonathan Dawson

Hey Dad! (TV) Gary Reilly Prods/Seven Network 1987–
Executive Producer: Gary Reilly
Producers/writers/directors: Various

Homicide (TV) Crawford Productions 1960s
Executive Producer: Hector Crawford
Producers/writers/directors: Various

The Jagged Edge (Film) Columbia 1985
Producer: Martin Ransahoff
Writer: Joe Esztherhas
Director: Richard Marquand

Joh's Jury (TV) Southern Star/ABC 1992
Producer: Rod Allan
Writer: Ian David
Director: Ken Cameron

Lethal Weapon (Film) Warner Bros/Silver Pictures 1987
Producer: Richard Donner/Joel Silver
Writer: Shane Black
Director: Richard Donner

The Little Shop of Horrors (Film) Warner Bros 1986
Producer: David Geffen
Writer: Howard Ashman
Director: Frank Oz

Lorenzo's Oil (Film) Universal/Kennedy Miller 1992
Producer: Doug Mitchell/George Miller
Writer: George Miller/Nick Enright
Director: George Miller

Malcolm (Film) Cascade Films/Hoyts 1986
Producer: Nadia Tass/David Parker
Writer: David Parker
Director: Nadia Tass

Neighbours (TV) Grundy Organisation 1985–
Producers/writers/directors: Various

North by Northwest (Film) MGM 1959
Producer: Alfred Hitchcock
Writer: Ernest Lehman
Director: Alfred Hitchcock

On Golden Pond (Film) ITC Films/IFC Films 1981
Producer: Bruce Gilbert
Writer: Ernest Thompson

Director: Mark Rydell

Outland (Film) Warner Bros/The Ladd Company 1981
Producer: Richard A. Roth
Writer: Peter Hyams
Director: Peter Hyams

The Piano (Film) Jan Chapman Productions 1993
Producer: Jan Chapman
Writer: Jane Campion
Director: Jane Campion

Presumed Innocent (Film) Warner Bros 1990
Producer: Sydney Pollack/Mark Rosenberg
Writer: Frank Pierson/Alan J. Pakula
Director: Alan J. Pakula

Prisoner (TV) Grundy Organisation/Network Ten 1979–86
Executive Producer: Reg Watson
Producers/writers/directors: Various

Proof (Film) Village Roadshow/House and Moorhouse 1991
Producer: Linda House
Writer: Jocelyn Moorhouse
Director: Jocelyn Moorhouse

Psycho (Film) Paramount 1960
Producer: Alfred Hitchcock
Writer: Robert Bloch
Director: Alfred Hitchcock

Rain Man (Film) United Artists/Guber-Peters 1988
Producer: Mark Johnson
Writer: Ronald Bass/Barry Morrow
Director: Barry Levinson

Rich and Famous (Film) MGM 1981
Producer: William Allyn
Writer: Gerald Ayres
Director: George Cukor

Rocky (Film) United Artists/Chartoff-Winkler Prods 1976
Producer: Robert Chartoff/Irwin Winkler
Writer: Sylvester Stallone
Director: John G. Avildsen

The Silence of the Lambs (Film) Orion 1991
Producer: Ken Utt/Edward Saxon/Ron Bozman
Writer: Ted Tally
Director: Jonathan Demme

Stanley and Iris (Film) MGM/Lantana 1989
Producer: Arlene Sellers/Alex Winitsky

Writer: Harriet Frank/Irving Ravetch Jnr
Director: Martin Ritt

Strictly Ballroom (Film)   Ronin Films/M&A Prods/Beyond Films 1992
Producer: Tristram Miall
Writer: Baz Luhrmann/Craig Pearce/Andrew Bouell
Director: Baz Luhrmann

Thelma and Louise (Film)   MGM/Percy Main Prods 1991
Producer: Ridley Scott/Mimi Polk
Writer: Callie Khouri
Director: Ridley Scott

Turtle Diary (Film)   United British Artists/British Lion Prods 1985
Producer: Richard Johnson
Writer: Harold Pinter
Director: John Irvin

Two for the Road (Film)   20th Century Fox 1967
Producer: Stanley Donen
Writer: Frederic Raphael
Director: Stanley Donen

Wall Street (Film)   20th Century Fox 1988
Producer: Edward R. Pressman
Writer: Stanley Weiser/Oliver Stone
Director: Oliver Stone

The Winds of War (TV)   Paramount 1983
Producer: Dan Curtis
Writer: Herman Wouk
Director: Dan Curtis

The Year My Voice Broke (Film)   Kennedy Miller 1987
Producer: George Miller/Doug Mitchell/Terry Hayes
Writer: John Duigan
Director: John Duigan

Bibliography

S. Field, *Screenplay: The foundations of screenwriting*, Dell Publishing, USA, 1979

——*The Screenwriter's workbook*, Dell Publishing, USA, 1984

L. Segar, *Making a Good Script Great*, Samuel French, Hollywood, USA, 1987

Index

formats in, 18–23; networks,
153–4; production of, 4;
treatment in, 102–3
tentative cuts, 104
themes, 135
three-act structure, 58, 59,
60–72; for television, 75–7, 80
thrillers, 12, 15–16, 68
thrust, 66
treatment, 101–3
triumphs, 14
turning points, 60–2, 121–3
Turtle Diary, 50, 51
tweaking of scripts, 127–8
Two for the Road, 84

understanding, 48

viability, 4
Victoria College of the Arts, 57
vignettes, 70
voice-overs, 111
voices, 82–5

Wall Street, 135
Williamson, David, 9
Winds of War, 9
writers, 3; fees of, 9; wants and
needs of, 24–5, 30
writing: action, 111–12; for
oneself, 3; for television, 5–6